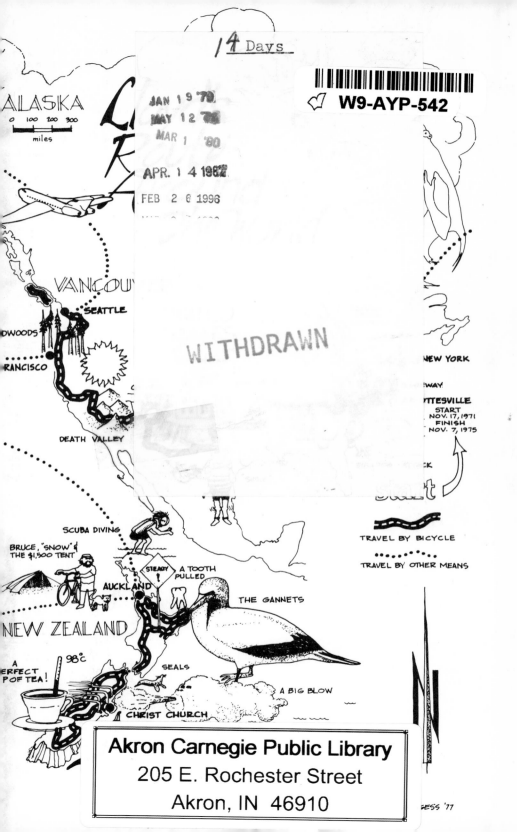

14 Days

ALASKA

0 100 200 300
miles

VANCOUVER

SEATTLE

REDWOODS

SAN FRANCISCO

DEATH VALLEY

NEW YORK

CHARLOTTESVILLE
START
NOV. 17, 1971
FINISH
NOV. 7, 1975

TRAVEL BY BICYCLE

TRAVEL BY OTHER MEANS

SCUBA DIVING

BRUCE, "SNOW" &
THE $1,500 TENT

STEADY

A TOOTH
PULLED

AUCKLAND

THE GANNETS

NEW ZEALAND

A PERFECT
CUP OF TEA!

98°C

SEALS

A BIG BLOW

CHRIST CHURCH

BURGESS '77

The Long Ride

by Lloyd Sumner
Introduction by Robert G. Deindorfer

Early one morning in November of 1971, Lloyd Sumner pedaled his bicycle due west from Charlottesville, Virginia in pursuit of a persistent dream—to travel the world under his own power. The fulfillment of this dream became one of the epic adventures in modern travel.

Four years later when Sumner finally returned home to Virginia, the odometer on his bike read 28,477.9 miles. What Lloyd had done was wheel around the world—with some help across the oceans and an occasional lift from an elephant, ostrich, or some other unusual transport.

As if his long ride was not challenging enough, he explored along the way the depths of Australia's Great Barrier Reef, climbed the summits of McKinley, Blanc, and Kilimanjaro, criss-crossed thick jungles, open seas, monsoons, volcanoes, north country tundra, African plains, and boiling bush country. Better still, he experienced all this on his own terms, pausing whenever he chose to, spinning his wheels when he felt it was time to travel on.

This is the true, detailed account of a young American who was not an experienced cyclist to begin with, but who had the courage, will, and stamina

(Continued on back flap)

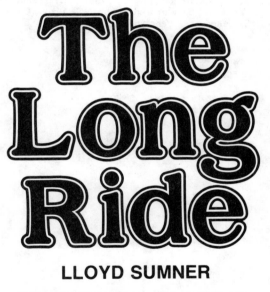

The Long Ride

LLOYD SUMNER

Introduction by Robert G. Deindorfer

STACKPOLE BOOKS

THE LONG RIDE
Copyright © 1978 by
Lloyd Sumner

Published by
STACKPOLE BOOKS
Cameron and Kelker Streets
P.O. Box 1831
Harrisburg, Pa. 17105

First printing, April 1978
Second printing, September 1978

Published simultaneously in Don Mills, Ontario, Canada
by Thomas Nelson & Sons, Ltd.

Printed in the U.S.A.

Library of Congress Cataloging in Publication Data

Sumner, Lloyd.
  The long ride.

  1. Sumner, Lloyd. 2. Voyages around the world.
I. Title.
G440.S9S93   1978   910'.41 [B]   77-28192
ISBN 0-8117-0952-3

Contents

Introduction

By Robert G. Deindorfer

During a casual conversation at the Explorers Club in New York City a vagabond member who has traveled the world out beyond God's back from Tasmania to Timbuktu was asked whether our venturesome old spirit has diminished. He studied the question briefly.

"It's gone, gone," he said. "Nobody seems to care any more."

"Nobody?" The shape of an audacious pedal-pushing exception spun in my mind. "Well, almost nobody. People don't have that same fever to step off into the unknown."

While the elderly man whose views had been solicited was guilty of some exaggeration, his basic message can be laid down in iron. It's perfectly true that few people are anxious to step off into the unknown these days strictly for the sake of adventure. Hedged in by convention, gorged on the vicarious wonders to be seen on television, increasingly apprehensive about a world so plainly out of joint, the contemporary definition of life in the raw generally comes down to a cookout in the backyard.

Like it or not, the bittersweet situation reflects a trend that has been gathering for a long time. Over a period of years, decades, even centuries, people have become less venturesome, more rooted to familiar places, victims of the new technology, trapped in great urban grids where they feed on fast food lunches, wrap themselves in the security blanket of jobs many of them don't really enjoy, hurry to catch the 5:24 for an evening of by-the-numbers television, without ever letting out a mutinous shriek.

7

There was a time when a large number of Americans did lead more venturesome lives, of course, if only because they had little or no choice. A raw new nation had to be opened for business, its land settled, its mass cobbled with steel rails, its frontiers hammered away. If the challenge involved attendant hazards, that was simply the way things were.

Yet long after the sod-busters settled Idaho, the last wagon trains wound into the sunset, the bolder among them managed to successfully scratch their itch for excitement in other ways. Back in my own lost midwestern boyhood, all too many years ago, for instance, we participated some ourselves, although naturally the thrills were scaled to size. We used to explore big caves whose dark winding tunnels scared us stiff, raft wide rivers without always knowing quite what lay ahead, tent in woods so deep those tingling night noises had to be—in the film of our imagination, anyway—bobcats, rattlers or bears.

"It's gone, gone," the man from the Explorers Club lamented.

And so it has. In a homogenized, split-level age the old juices rise no more. We are stuffed, stuffed and jaded, our sense of wonder blotted out by ringside seats for all too many live color spectaculars. Without leaving the comfort of our living room we spin the dial to riots and wars, mountain climbs and deep sea adventures, big game hunts and lunar landings.

In these circumstances, an audacious pedal-pushing exception named Lloyd Sumner amounts to a genuine throwback, an endangered species, a dated symbol of what we once were. Despite the profusion of plastic substitutes to be had, he still insists on the real thing. For reasons Sumner himself sometimes can't quite fathom, he chooses to absorb his adventure personally instead of vicariously.

Lloyd Sumner isn't cast in the heroic mold of song and legend. At the age of 34 he's fairly ordinary looking, in fact, with brown hair and bland, blank features, quiet, sometimes almost withdrawn, a typical off-the-rack, size 37 American, except for his accent, which is softened with the honey of his native Virginia. Altogether, he seems a perfect face in the crowd.

Yet at bottom Lloyd Sumner is a durable nomad who's tough as they come. Among other things, he can tote a 60-pound backpack, spin a bicycle more than 100 miles a day, scull boats, climb mountains, rough it in either tropical or Arctic conditions, read a pocket compass, trek all day long without any more fuel than an apple or a candy bar. It's just as well he's up to routinely managing burdens such as these, else he couldn't possibly have survived the adventure he embarked upon in the autumn of 1971.

What Sumner set out to do was to ride a bicycle around the world. A vagrant daydream? Not for Sumner. Along with the bike, camping kit and $200 in cash, he was fortified with an iron resolve, lively curiosity and a background of years out in the woods and waters the day he started wheeling west with the sun from Charlottesville.

Predictably, however, a number of friends thought Sumner wasn't up to the challenge despite his impressive qualifications. He didn't speak the languages prevalent in most of the lands he would be traveling, he didn't have sufficient emergency funds in case of a flat-out crisis, he wasn't fully aware of the malevolent backcountry he would encounter, especially through the Asian land mass and in Africa. But as one friend told him, a successful ride as far as the west coast of America, if he got that far, would be a great memory he could feed on for years to come—and hence, presumably, he ought to settle for that manageable, if impressive, distance.

As things turned out, Sumner kept right on going once he reached the western limits of the continental United States. He fanned north for the sake of an epic mountain climb in Alaska, where he kept company with a native girl he seemed to enjoy—reading between the lines—more than he cares to admit. He reached for Hawaii, explored New Zealand and Australia with the same zeal he was to show throughout his odyssey, pushed on to Java, Sumatra, Thailand, Nepal and India, wheeled down the rim of Africa.

Along the way the bold young southerner savored the assorted flavors of a world in ferment. While he invariably preferred open space to the urban crowds, he chose to sleep in jailhouses and with native families, forsake cola drinks for whatever the indigenous beverage happened to be, ride for hours and days off the beaten track in search of a stray temple, a particular waterfall, a patch of jungle said to thrum with big game animals he hadn't seen before.

Sumner was faithful to the bike he rode across the continents, faithful even when the spokes rusted onto the wheels and home-cooked patches melted off the tires in the brooding tropics, and yet he seldom refused the opportunity to test-drive some other form of transit, if only because it was different, which was the point of his trip, as it used to be for other adventurers who set out to see the world. In Australia he signed on as a member of the crew on an expensive yacht bound for far places, before the owner died in his arms and he was marooned on a tropical island. In South Africa he rode an ostrich, which, while irregular, wasn't the first wildlife he'd used to cover a distance.

Hear him: "Circling the airport during an easy descent, we watched men, women and children drive their cattle off the long grass runway.

Since the luxury hotel the flimflam man back in Kathmandu had so lyrically described was served only from this remote airport, I guessed private cars would be awaiting us. The pilot, smiling at my innocence, pointed to the south. Our transportation was right on schedule— elephants, three elephants, swaying over the meadow, a mahout/ chauffeur aboard each one."

Any time Sumner the free spirit was asked to resolve a choice of two options, one of them familiar and relatively safe, the other a step into the void, he chose the unknown. Show him a mountain: he wanted to climb it. Point out a paved road and a track through the bush: he opted for the bush. Show him a comfortable, western-style hotel and a wattle shelter deep in the jungle: the wattle shelter won hands down.

In a way, that itch to travel the byways, that willingness to avoid the creature comforts, that very boldness almost did him in not once but several times. A leopard stalked him in Sumatra without ever making a meal of Sumner, a rhinoceros charged his party as he rode an elephant in Nepal, another elephant abruptly gone haywire went trumpeting up a road in southern Thailand in harrowing pursuit of him.

Better still, Sumner has the ability to describe these and his other extraordinary experiences with a vivid clarity and a special eye for detail. When he fixes on a witch doctor who cured him of the mysterious tropical disease accompanied by a 106-degree temperature he was suffering, we can feel, smell and picture exactly how it was, ringside spectators focusing in on a minor miracle.

He finally rode his bike back home to Virginia with 28,478 miles showing on the clock after nearly four years. Everyone who reads his *The Long Ride* will have the same mingled feelings he did that special day. We celebrate his incredible accomplishment, mourn the fact that it is over and done with.

More than anything else, Sumner's book illustrates the dramatic differences between the author and his audience. He amounts to an original who rode for miles to see the sunset melt down over a particular roll of hills in Sumatra. And we are status quo seekers locked in the more comfortable, less dauntless boundaries of our vicarious time. But at least we can join Lloyd Sumner, bless him, on his twirling, flavorful ride round the raggedy edges of a world we are all too timid to really see for ourselves.

The Beginning

At dawn the trip began. An epic trip of some sort had been spinning in my mind for weeks, months, years, in fact, mute and constant, taking on more excitement the more I got to brooding on it, always enlarging instead of fading, the whole thing clear as a bell only a few weeks before. And at dawn on November 17, 1971, I set out to cash in the vague dream I had been dreaming for so long.

Perhaps I was acting hastily. Perhaps I should have trained hard, studied repair books, read texts on touring, enrolled in language courses. But I figured to train and learn while I traveled. Even if I spoke some French, German, Italian, Spanish and Japanese, these languages wouldn't be negotiable in Java, Thailand, Nepal or Malawi. Somehow it would be more practical if I mastered the subtle art of nonverbal communication.

Perhaps I was acting hastily by starting in the dead of winter too, not properly equipped, unaware of basic techniques to steer by, with a total of only $200 cash in my pocket. But I was admittedly a rookie rolling onto a long and bewildering track—and I might just as well start as an innocent and hope for the best.

That last week was inevitably crowded with all the little things a person committed to a major trip must suffer. I fanned through maps and brochures, visited friends, relatives and university associates for potluck farewells, and, finally, packed, which took a little doing.

As I sorted through my modest belongings—I've always had less of the world's goods than most—I decided that the most effective approach would be to segregate them in three separate piles. The things in one stack would be thrown or given away, the contents of the second would be stored with a sister who lived close by and was helping me in every way she could.

What went into the third stack were essentials I might want to take with me, only it kept growing and growing despite the fact that I'm a hardscrabble man given to acquiring necessities instead of luxuries. Still, when it came time for a final selection I couldn't bear leaving anything behind. In it all went, tent, sleeping bag, cooking gear, cameras, spare clothes, climbing kit, extra shoes, more than fifty pounds of equipment, stowed in saddlebags and a summit pack. Right or wrong, I was operating on pure gut reflex: If it fits, take it along.

It wasn't as if I was a novice packing for my first overnight trip, either. I'd been an outdoorsman for years, for as long as I can remember, back through a long coil of time. In the rolling Virginia countryside I still love beyond anything else, I'd walked crooked trails leading nowhere in particular, fished backland streams for bass, bream and catfish, rigged lean-to shelters, climbed the slopes, rafted rivers, sustained myself with whatever I could confect over an open cooking fire.

I'd been an outdoorsman on a relatively short leash ever since my heels first started to itch as a boy. I'd traveled, hiked, camped and grown accustomed to the elements in and around my various Virginia homes without ever quite putting a Lloyd Sumner show on a truly long road.

Yet the urge to do precisely that had been rubbing at my nerve ends for a long time. I fiddled with the idea during many a regional campout, fiddled with the idea through the dead of several winters. In the end I reminded myself of the couplet from Goethe:

> Whatever you can do, or dream you can, begin it. Boldness has genius, power, and magic in it.

Personally, I felt that I had an abundance of boldness, if not the genius, power and magic others seem blessed with. Good friends aware of the fact that such virtues are in short supply in my case couldn't help but question the concept of my bulging aspiration. Their queries, none of them designed to be cruel or abusive, were right to the point.

"Are you in shape?" one of them asked.

"No." I couldn't lie. "Not really."

At the age of twenty-eight I was five-seven, 150 pounds, not especially athletic, not in terms of competitive sports, anyway, wiry without being muscular, adequately coordinated without being so reflexed

I could hit a moonbeam at so many yards. I was and am a standard-issue American, somewhat smallish, in good health but in no way shaped to stand out in a crowd. No, I wasn't really in shape.

"And what foreign languages do you speak?" Another put what he knew to be a rhetorical question.

"Come, come," I said. "You know exactly how many foreign languages I speak. None."

It wasn't that these friends were trying to discourage me by exposing some inadequacies. As friends they simply wanted to document the realities, do up an inventory of practical credits and debits, make me realize that I might be getting into a situation I couldn't always cope with.

"Just what do you know about bicycle touring?" An especially close buddy named John looked me straight in the eye the first time we started barbering on the subject.

"Not much." On reflection, a downward qualification seemed in order. "Nothing, really."

Whatever specific questions acquaintances raised as the days dwindled down, there was another, more significant aspect they couldn't fathom. Neither could I when I considered it, although the very fact that I was so wonderfully comfortable and contented may have contributed to my decision to shake my life up.

The summer of 1971 was a time of great satisfaction for me. I had achieved what I considered an idyllic existence. I created original art by computer, which was something new in our increasingly technological age, and I lectured a bit. I sold the art directly and by catalog. Between the computer art and the lectures I was able to earn enough in a single month to survive a full year at the modest level I enjoyed.

I lived at Ridgeway, a lovely old colonial house standing amidst rolling Virginia hills, almost a mile off the nearest highway, which was nice, but within easy reach of the cultural, educational and sports opportunities to be had in Charlottesville. For my rent I worked on the estate for a few hours each month. For some of my food I sharecropped a kitchen garden with my landlord. There was a pond to swim, spirited horses to ride, woods to walk, open sky to contemplate.

Yet I sorted through the third stack of personal belongings, balled them up, fitted them into the pack and the saddlebags with no regret. I was perfectly happy right there in Virginia, happier than most people, I suspect, but I had this irresistible urge beating at me to enlarge my focus.

By nature I am a fairly inquisitive person. I like to know what makes things tick. If this curiosity involves traveling a distance, riffling through reference books, asking questions or trying something new for myself, so much the better. I'm no great explorer in the sense that Columbus was an explorer when he sought out new lands for spices and gold, but I happen to be a homemade explorer. What I generally explore is the prospect of a more satisfying life.

In this particular exploration I was about to set out upon I hoped the economics wouldn't be beyond me. I decided to start with only $200 cash in my pocket—and another $1,000 in reserve in the bank. In case of an accident, illness or depression I could always draw on that $1,000, which was enough to bring me back home.

Meanwhile, I would use the sleeping bag and tent as shelter wherever I could, live off the land if and when its bounty included edible foods, replenish my cash funds by sending an occasional story back to *The Daily Progress*, lecturing and doing computer art along the way and hoping that another sister who agreed to handle the sales of my inventory of art would register some sales in my absence. Two hundred dollars cash admittedly wasn't very much to start traveling a great distance, but I hoped it would prove to be adequate seed money, unless I encountered some terrible calamity, which almost happened several times.

In the peaceful cool of the Virginia evenings that last week before I finally pushed off I couldn't pull the shades of the future. I had no way of knowing I was to come upon treacherous mud that would almost suck me down, powdery sand that burned the eyes, phantom tracks that disappeared in the thick heart of the jungle. I didn't anticipate various dogs snapping at my legs, malevolent drivers aiming their big trucks straight at me, a rogue elephant chasing me for three miles.

In the cool of Virginia I never foresaw heat so oppressive that it hit me like a wall and melted the patches off my tires. I didn't predict a ripped Achilles tendon, a tropical disease that inflated my temperature to 106 degrees, melancholy times when I wondered whether the trip was worth it.

Other moments had an edge of menace to them, too. A reverse current was to bushwhack me, drive me into turbulent open seas during a skin dive. A twilight struggle over a glacial moraine 16,000 feet high was scheduled to save a fellow climber. Despite my lifelong fondness for animals, a leopard was to stalk me, a camel to bite into my arm, a wild boar to rip at me with long cruel tusks.

I couldn't possibly anticipate a bittersweet night scented with promise that turned terribly sour. In a scene straight out of *Easy Rider*

Leaving Ridgeway on 17 November 1971 to begin a bicycle trip around the world

a carload of drunks, every one of them hellbent on violence, lurched through a black western night, straight for my solitary camp.

Before I began I had no idea of the perils, the wonders, the excitement, and the deep-down satisfaction that I would experience in the next four years of my life. I knew it would be memorable without ever knowing exactly how memorable it was to be. All I knew for sure those last few days was that it was time to get on with it.

I couldn't sleep. All that last night I kept rearranging my body, twisting and wondering, my senses beating, my mind wildly alive. I had a thousand questions, a thousand doubts. After all the vague dreams, after finally resolving exactly what it was I wanted, the prospects of the trip itself set me to brooding as never before. I was scared.

But at dawn on November 17, 1971, I tightened a loose saddlebag, felt the bulge of that $200 in my pocket, climbed on a bicycle determined to ride at least 24,901 miles (the exact distance around the earth at the equator) around a world thrumming with I didn't know what, except for its strangeness to me.

Chapter 1

United States East

The bike rolled down the broad front lawn of Ridgeway, bumping some, slowly gathering speed, wheels squishing on the frosted grass. I turned for a last look. My eyes clouded over briefly, and I blinked, blinked hard before I spun onto Va. 20 the first day of my global tour.

In the cool of the morning I twined round a bend in the road, and another, the past abruptly fading away, a memory to lean on in the weeks and months ahead. Traffic in Charlottesville was thicker than usual, the bike wobbled under its heavy load. To the south every roll of hill seemed longer, steeper, more agonizing than the last. A flicker of pain throbbed in the small of my back, growing as the miles stretched, an ominous beginning for so long a projected trip.

That first day I had assigned myself eighty-two miles, the distance to Lynchburg, where my friends Sam and Louise Gamble were standing by, expecting me as an overnight guest whenever I managed to make it. Eighty-two miles might not seem like much. But I'd never cycled over sixty miles in any one day before, and never with a fifty-pound load straining an old bike rusted by five years of duty carrying me around Charlottesville.

Before long it was apparent that the old-timer wasn't up to a global tour. Maybe I wasn't up to it, either. But I'd have to make do with myself. The bike was replaceable, as I had known all along. I'd ordered a Schwinn Super Sport, which, being in short supply due to the current two-wheeler fad, I was to collect along the way three weeks hence.

Even after my back started to ache on U.S. 29 I never questioned
the type of transport I had chosen. The advantages of a bicycle instead
of a motorcycle, a car or even my thumb were abundantly clear. It
was cheap and healthy, despite the bulging pain in my back. It was
easy to fix, easy to hide for any side trips I wanted to take afoot, easy
to pack on an airplane or a ship when it came time to cross a sheet of
water.

In an age of audible clatter and polluted air the bike amounts to a
refreshing alternative to newer, more complicated vehicles. It makes
no noise beyond an audible gasping as I ascend steeper slopes, creates
and emits no pollutants. As a dedicated environmentalist, I care about
these contemporary curses.

Apart from the elemental simplicity of a bike, its wide-open character enabled me to tune in the changing flavors wherever I rode. I'd
be able to see, hear, even smell and feel the experiences I came upon,
which, while not always a blessing, as I was to learn, at least offered a
full-dimensional scope of people, places and things. The people themselves probably would be friendlier and more hospitable too, if only
because a stranger on pedals was operating at approximately their
pace, instead of hurtling past behind glass in a motorcar or van.

Trucks blasted by, an edge of head wind slowed me down. On ahead
the hills seemed to rise higher and higher, formidable swells lighted in
sunshine, challenges to test me for the future, whatever that might
bring. Like an old-fashioned baseball manager, I was playing them one
day at a time in the beginning, Lynchburg the first day, if my aching
back didn't let go, anyway, more mileage the following day.

According to a hazy plan I had concocted I would ride west across
the United States first, to get the hang of cycling in relatively familiar
surroundings. Once I reached the continental limits I would pack on to
Australia and New Zealand, strange new lands for me, no doubt about
it, but new lands where the language and culture were much the same,
before I was tough enough to spin into the unknown.

According to that same hazy plan, I would travel at the pace I
wanted and remain utterly flexible. If I wanted to linger somewhere
for a while, I'd linger long as I chose. If I wanted to detour to canoe a
river, ski a snowfield or plumb the inside of a cave, I'd do just that.
As a climber with a yen to scale peaks far higher than I had been exposed to in Virginia, I'd climb whatever excited me.

One other caveat lay fixed in my mind. I had a tremendous urge to
cycle around the world, the whole blinking world, but if I saw that
it got too much, or if I wasn't enjoying myself, I would simply let go
and come home again. So even my ultimate goal could be scaled to size.

"If you make it as far as the Mississippi River, fine," a friend had said. "If you make it to California, hurrah. Either one is a great achievement. Just do the best you can."

But the despair I felt pumping up the hills that first day put a crimp in my dream. My energy tailed off, my muscles throbbed. I squinted into the setting sun and inhaled a heavy cloud of carbon monoxide. Somehow that fueled the fires of fatigue and pain crackling inside me. All of a sudden I asked myself some tough questions. Is this what I want for the next few years? Don't I have any better sense? Only a blind cussed stubbornness drove me on, on over the roadway, on over the hellish hills, on to Lynchburg.

I sprawled out on the floor in the Gambles' living room, gasping, holding my sides, so worn I nearly fainted. But my friends had exactly the proper prescription for my assorted aches and pains. They tipped me into a bed, pointed to a hot bath, served up a dinner featuring fresh-caught fish. I felt almost human again. Maybe, just maybe, I'd try it for another day.

I left something more than a thank-you note with Louise and Sam Gamble there in Lynchburg. I also left my stove, a fuel bottle, a cooking pot, a radio, a spare tire and some extra clothes, which weighed a total of fifteen pounds I could do without. After only a day on the road I was learning to travel light as a Tuareg.

On the country road curving toward Alta Vista my doubts of the day before faded away. Bicycling a distance was great stuff, serene and isolated, especially with that surplus fifteen pounds behind. Small farms and great estates, country stores and unspoiled villages appeared as the miles unwound. The pain in my back had disappeared, and the temperature was dead right for pumping a bike. That second morning I knew that I could make it clear to the Mississippi—and maybe even beyond.

For the next two weeks I rode a crazyquilt pattern stopping with friends and relatives who had offered me room and board. Gradually I adjusted to the nomadic life, just as I had hoped. My on-the-saddle training course wiped out any lingering regrets that I hadn't read guidebooks on cycling, taken a do-it-yourself repair course, trained harder and even enrolled in language classes before the tour began. I was happy—and learning to cope with minor emergencies as they appeared.

In Greensboro, North Carolina a reporter for the local newspaper hit it about right. "Somehow Lloyd Sumner does not fit the mind's eye of an adventurer, at least not to the mind's picture of TV and movie adventurers," he wrote. "He's just a little guy with short sandy hair and an easy smile. Unassuming and quiet spoken." Well, all right. I guess I am.

I fixed my first flat tire on a long mountain pass. I didn't fix it with the lockstep speed of a professional repairman, of course, but I did manage, which was all I had hoped. It was so cold that day my water bottle froze and broke. Six inches of fresh snow lay on the back roads, causing me to skid some, but I passed that test too, although the weather did slow me down.

Back over the line in lower Virginia again, I cycled past the rolling farm where I was born the last of thirteen children. Vagrant old memories stirred. I saw the homemade golf course I had cut for myself, the greens grown over, the fairways now no more. I saw the slope where I made my first ski jump in an awkward tangle of arms and legs. I saw the fields I had worked from the age of four until my mother and father, good honest people, died when I was sixteen. The old farm still had the power to stir me, as it does to this day.

I was brooding on my lost boyhood there at the family farm outside Fancy Gap when scraps of old conversation came back. My father was a settled man with few interests other than his farm, his family and his church, but he had been a rover when he was younger. He used to tell me how he hopped freights to go west in 1915, how he had been accidentally locked in a boxcar loaded with beans for five days, how he had to flatten beside the tracks with a train passing only inches away the time he was trapped in a tunnel. So I'd come by my itch for far places naturally.

Several brothers and sisters I visited in and around Fancy Gap expressed mixed feelings about the wisdom of such an ambitious, time-consuming trip. But all of them had talked it up in conversations with their friends and neighbors. One neighbor insisted my brother buy me a handgun and a rearview mirror. I refused both. I was safer without a handgun, and I didn't want to know what was behind me.

I rode my lame duck old bike on to Salem when I got word the new one was awaiting me. It was green and sleek, an impressive-looking machine that seemed up to a spin around the world, if I was. Somehow it seemed to need a proper name. I named it Maria for no particular reason except for the fact that the two of us would go wherever the breezes took us. It struck me as good a name as any.

But Maria and I didn't take to each other immediately. The new bike was jerky, bumpy, loose. Maybe Schwinn had built its Super Sport for little old ladies who'd drive it at moderate speeds only on Sundays. On the steep slopes and rough roads winding up the Appalachian Mountains I had more trouble adjusting to Maria than I guessed I would. Slack mountain people not especially fond of cyclists anyway didn't make things any easier.

After two days of hard riding I made camp in a raging storm almost a mile high on the Trail of the Lonesome Pine on the Virginia-Kentucky line. A day later I had to splint a broken rear luggage carrier with an empty beer can I found along the road. But the damaged support broke a spoke in the rear wheel, the wheel gradually warped, the tire blew completely off the rim.

Moments later the other carrier support broke, too. I splinted it but now my heels hit the saddlebags every revolution unless I bent my ankles sharply. The bending of my ankles caused the Achilles tendons on both heels to become so sore that I was barely able to walk. A prolonged time-out was required before any further cycling commenced.

Bicycling in snow near Fancy Gap, Virginia

While recuperating to a point where I could pick up the tour again, I joined some friends for a week of canoeing in the Okefenokee Swamp and then piled up savings by lecturing on computer art in Ottawa, Cincinnati and Upland, Indiana. The speeches were beamed to a basic presentation. I opened with family audience type jokes, offered my rationale for computer-assisted drawings as genuine art, displayed color slides of various drawings. Enthusiastic crowds of art students, computer professionals and computer science students warmed me every bit as much as the checks for those lectures.

In Upland I had the good fortune to meet Bob Davenport, a former All-American fullback from UCLA and current director of The Wandering Wheels, a band of long-distance cyclists at Taylor University. Davenport takes a dim view of at least one aspect of modern times. He feels many problems afflicting American youth are caused by what he describes as an "adventure gap."

"Youngsters need adventure," he told me. "Adventure is a challenge, a test, a way of stretching your potential. It can't be satisfied by dialing in superheroes on television or by organized sports one afternoon every week or so. It has to be found out in the field."

Davenport gave me a Wandering Wheels safety flag for my trip. It was a fluorescent orange banner attached to a five-foot fiberglass staff. The first thing I did when my ankles finally healed and I pulled the bicycle out of a garage in Richmond, Kentucky was to fly the colors in hopes they would be seen more quickly by drivers in traffic or hilly country.

Beyond My Old Kentucky Home State Park near Bardstown, with the bike running smoothly and my ankles causing no pain, I put the flagstaff to practical use. On a back road in strip-mine country three vicious, full-grown but half-starved bulldogs charged me, barking, closing in from both sides, snapping at my legs. I jerked the flagstaff out, hammered the closest dog in the head, knocked him off balance.

With the other two moving in from both flanks, I had serious fears that I might cease to be. I rammed the staff at the dog on my right, swung it across the handlebar to fend off the other. His teeth sunk in the saddlebag and the bike wobbled off the road. My heart pounding, my arm swinging in an effort to keep the fangs out of my leg, I desperately tried to regain control and put on some speed. If I was going to the dogs, I'd give it my best shot.

All of a sudden a scruffy-looking man loomed on the road ahead of me. The dogs kept barking, just out of range of the staff. Somewhere behind me a hostile voice, hard and ugly, passed the word.

"Cut him off! Cut him off, Mike!"

An irate dog owner was all I needed. Backwoods people in that coal-mining area had a reputation for closeness, for meanness, for hostility to outsiders. I found myself in a double jeopardy situation, angry dogs and angry natives. But as I zipped past, the lead man stepped aside with only a soft question.

"Why didn't you kick the shit out of them dogs?" he drawled.

At sunset that day my odometer showed over 100 miles—my first century—with no peaceful campsite yet in view. A few miles later a cemetery stood on a hillside. Why not? After all, the word means "sleeping place" in the original Greek. I was too tired to pitch the tent. I crawled in the sleeping bag, slept the long night amidst granite head-stones in that Kentucky cemetery.

Next day both Maria and I had our troubles. The rear carrier and four spokes broke, my heels began to throb with pain again. In Padu-cah, Kentucky a repairman who replaced the spokes blamed it on a bent frame. I wondered whether I could blame the heel miseries on my own bent frame.

In Paducah I was also booked for an interview program on the local television station. The interlocutor, while agreeably friendly and in-quisitive, expressed a blank ignorance on the purpose of my trip.

"What on earth would cause an otherwise normal human being to take three years out of his life to bicycle around the world?" he asked.

As I pedaled on west it struck me that there was no satisfactory answer to a loaded question so rigid as that. A person either understood or he didn't. In my view I was in no way losing three years of my life. With any luck I would do more living, more real living, in the next three years than many Americans, even talk-show television hosts in Kentucky, managed to stack up in a lifetime.

On Sunday it rained steadily, but the weather didn't diminish an erupting thrill. Up on a long narrow bridge I saw the thick swollen muddy flow of the Mississippi wash far below me. I had reached my first important checkpoint, which a number of friends had doubted I would ever reach. If I wasn't exactly going strong, at least I was still going, which was the next best thing.

People down in the Ozarks turned out to be an unpredictable lot. One man stopped to invite me to his family's Sunday dinner, three kinds of meat and eleven varieties of vegetable, all grown on the farm. And a day later I was about to shop at a country store when one of the loungers out front heaved a fist-sized rock at me without any warning.

Down through southern Missouri and Arkansas the choppy roads subjected my body to a constant jarring. The pain in my heels was hard to bear. In an effort to gain some relief I tied the toe clips tight and propelled entirely on the upstroke. In Doniphan I gave myself a full day off, although I was little better the next morning and managed only a few miles to the Narrows.

I camped a half-mile off the road in a clump of trees that seemed well hidden. In the dark of the night I awakened to the drum of footsteps approaching my camp. A voice, friendly but unfamiliar, rose in the void.

"Mister Sumner in there?"

"What do you want?" I asked.

"I have a young lady here who wants to meet you."

Well, you never know. Bewildered by the intrusion, I dressed, crawled from the tent, met a big comfortable man named Ray Morse and his dark-haired, nine-year-old daughter. They couldn't have been nicer. He explained his visit while I rebuilt the fire.

"Over in Doniphan I heard you were in the area and liked canoeing," he said. "It would be a shame if you left here without seeing our lovely rivers. Well, I've brought my canoe along. You can load your bike aboard and come down to my farm in Arkansas tomorrow."

The Eleven Point River coiled through peaceful country rolling off into hills. It was refreshing to be paddling instead of pedaling for a few miles. When I reached the Morse farm he hit the high spots of his new lifeway as we gathered a load of wood. Not satisfied with his career as an aerospace engineer, he had quit his job, packed up his wife and two children and settled on a small farm in rural Arkansas where he hoped to live happily ever afterwards.

Further along the backcountry roads the next day I found that I couldn't walk without a limp. My heels were as bad as they'd been in Kentucky, maybe worse. No matter how much I tried to screw up my spirits I had an unholy fear that my yearning adventure would end before reaching my next goal, the Continental Divide. But I decided to keep pumping west until I actually fell off the bike.

I fell off the bike in eastern Oklahoma shifting into high gear, when the drive chain wedged between the front sprocket and the chain guard. Instead of stopping to effect a simple repair, I tried to free the chain while coasting at nearly twenty-five miles an hour, which was a blunder, a painful blunder, as I discovered tumbling onto a gravel shoulder in the road, cut, bruised, feeling the shock of my first wreck.

That experience convinced me I had better trade the bike in for a more durable model if and when we made it to Norman, Oklahoma. Meanwhile, I hobbled into the typically informal western village of Dustin, cleaned and bandaged my wounds, spent the night in the local jail, at the invitation, not the official insistence, understand, of the sheriff.

I must have ridden a mile or so down the road next morning before it struck me that I'd left my flagstaff behind. Only the jail was shut tight and the sheriff nowhere to be found when I returned. Impatient to get on, I forced an entry in a window someone had forgotten to lock, which must have made me one of the few people who ever broke *into* a jail.

Rolling toward Norman, wondering what sort of a trade-in I might get for a new bicycle, an amazing transformation unfolded. Slowly, slowly, then with greater emphasis, I started to feel better. The various aches, the knot in my lower back, even the screaming pain in my heels deflated to where I could barely feel them, lost in transit somewhere along the roadway, presumably, and I was soaring, riding beautifully, covering the distance, at peace with the picturesque outdoor life around me.

In Norman I took the bike to the Schwinn dealer in hopes it might be healed as miraculously as I was. The dealer put it on a rack, turned it upside down, said the problem was misaligned spokes. They were properly aligned there on the spot.

My heels completely recovered, running with a strong north wind, I broke every one of my records for speed and distance cycling south toward Texas. I rode 10 miles in 23 minutes, 24.5 miles in an hour, a total of 133 miles in an 8-hour day. On a flat stretch of road I even reached a speed of forty-one miles an hour, or enough to idly wonder whether a patrol car might tag me.

On that slant down into Texas Maria set a record, too. Eight spokes broke in 200 miles. If I hadn't been convinced before, I was now determined to trade bicycles by the time I reached Melissa, Texas. But a local dealer insisted—he put his reputation on the line, in fact—that the trouble was a defective hub. He put on a new wheel, a new handlebar bag, a new water bottle, several new cables, all of them generous gifts, his "contribution to a mighty adventure," as he put it in wishing me well.

In Texas I made a long detour to visit an old Sunday school teacher from my boyhood. Ruth Morse was somewhere up in her seventies, and yet she remained as active and caught up in an assortment of interests as ever. Among other things, she worked for the Red Cross, ran a poetry society and wrote a daily newspaper column.

For a gentle woman who admitted to being an overly protective mother, Mrs. Morse surprised me by explaining how the family had once rid itself of a large alligator sometimes seen dangerously close to their daughter's play area in the side yard. She tethered the daughter to a tree as live bait, waited for the 'gator to come make his move. As

Katie, the redhead, and Susie, the boa constrictor, near McKinney, Texas

the daughter cried out and the alligator approached what must have looked an easy meal, her husband resolved the worry forever by shooting it dead.

One morning a retired Army colonel drove out to the Morse farm to interview me for the local newspaper. He listened attentively, raised a number of astute questions and said he thought my long ride was in the tradition of our old American frontier spirit.

"I'm convinced you have got the guts to endure any hardship and the brains to get out of difficulty," he said. "But I do have this one concern. How the Sam Hill will you get out of Texas without losing your heart to these beautiful Texas women?"

As things turned out, it wasn't easy. I had been so very engrossed in the challenge of cycling that I'd almost—almost, I say—forgotten about feminine charms. But Katie, a brisk, bouncy red-headed daughter of a Dallas lawyer, proved the colonel had a good point. Katie and I went to art exhibits and museums, films and restaurants.

One day she surprised me with an invitation to meet a friend named Susie. We drove to the Heard Wildlife Sanctuary. Susie was long and fairly slender, with a complexion like a—well, she had the complexion of any other seven-foot boa constrictor. Katie coiled the golden yellow snake around her head with such assurance that I tentatively lifted Susie up, wound her on my neck and shoulders. Muscles strong enough to strangle relatively large animals strained and rippled harmlessly through the long body—an exciting feeling.

I never really had my fill of all the good company, the good food and the good comforts there in Texas. As the colonel had predicted, I was tempted to stay longer, mostly because of my friend Katie the redhead. But there were overriding considerations. I had already endured the bone-deep cold of an eastern winter. More than anything else, I wanted to avoid the blazing heat of a western summer.

Chapter 2

United States West

Ever since pioneers who filled wagon trains winding into the old West passed the word about snakes in general and rattlers in particular, Americans have acted downright skittish any time they hear a suspicious buzzing out in the wide open spaces, as well they might. It happens, not often, but often enough to keep the stretchers warm. However, I've never been nervous about poisonous snakes. Having studied the habits of snakes, I know the odds are very much in my favor.

On my ride out through west Texas winter turned into summer without so much of a sign of spring. Air in the flat, treeless land was hot and dry, shade was scarce, towns were frequently half a day apart. All I had to contend with was the weather, for endless distances, the dust storms—and the scorpions and rattlers friendly people along the way kept warning me about.

"Shouldn't stop on the desert," a leathery young man in Texas scolded me. "Snakes, rattlesnakes, they like to snuggle close to a person to seek warmth."

Several people presumably interested in my welfare went so far as to cite diabolic chapter and verse. According to one, he awakened to find a rattler coiled on his chest. He lay petrified for almost two hours, or so he told me, before his partner shot the snake at point-blank range when it raised its head and hissed. Another swore a rattler actually crawled into his sleeping bag at a time when it was being occupied by the owner.

Yet I camped on the desert at least twenty nights without so much as seeing a garter snake. So much for herpetology.

Now that the bicycle and I were both running well, the spin west into the sun was a pleasure. We passed oil wells and cotton fields, antelope and roadrunners, creaking windmills and working ranches, all under an enormous rim of sky in country that seemed endless. Frequently the plowed land ran off to the horizon in every direction, and there were few trees. But the tumbleweed, the sagebrush and the cactus had a splendor to it—and I loved the solitude! After all, it was part of my old hometown, planet Earth.

Despite the punishing weather I averaged more than 100 miles a day. As I spun through the heat, with the bike no longer throwing spokes, farmers waved from their tractors, small boys riding school buses smiled, agreeable men offered to buy me soft drinks in dusty village stores. If I generally chose a secluded campsite far off the road at night, it was only because I'd found that even the friendly universe stretching into the west included the normal quota of misfits.

One night I pitched my camp behind some bushes in the dark after riding long past sunset. Around midnight I was violently jolted awake. The ground shook, a deafening roar drummed in my ears, and a brilliant fireball blinded me. I didn't know whether it was a thunderstorm, an earthquake or the end of the world some religious cranks keep predicting. I lay rigid, my heart pumping hard, as a freight train thundered past an arm's length from where I lay.

Before I fell asleep again an old memory flickered. My father used to tell a story about the night he heard the rumble of an approaching train while he was walking on the bridge spanning a deep canyon. He slipped down between two cross ties and hung on for dear life until the train whooshed over him. But his arms were so numb he couldn't pull himself back up. He heard the sound of rushing water somewhere below him in the dark, held on for almost an hour. Finally he said his last prayers, let go and fell a matter of perhaps six inches. He had nearly reached the far side without realizing it.

Soon after crossing into New Mexico I met two dazzling California blondes, kindred spirits, both of them, riding their bikes toward New Orleans. We exchanged experiences, names and addresses.

"I hope you're carrying plenty of food and water," one of them said. "There is a stretch ahead where you won't find either for three days."

I was astonished. "Three days! Are you sure? My map doesn't show a stretch of three hundred miles between stops."

"Oh, do you ride that fast?" she said. "We only make ten to thirty miles a day."

Susan and Marsh, bicycling from Los Angeles to New Orleans, seen near Carlsbad, New Mexico

I parted with these kindred spirits of the trail sooner than I wanted. All too often it was like that. All too often I rode away from people I wanted to know better.

After 500 miles of flatland the Chihuahua Desert came as a relief, at least until I tried to sleep on it. The ground was covered with sharp rocks, dense vegetation, spiked cactus. The Matterhorn penetrated my left shoulder, and the entire Rocky Mountain Range dug into my right side. I rolled into some thorns somewhere in the middle of the night. Next day I found thorns in the bike's tires, another so firmly implanted in my leg that it didn't work loose for two weeks.

I had yet to see it in any cycling manuals, but I developed a prudent cure for riding through dust storms. What I did was close my windward eye, twist my head to leeward and pump as hard as I could, generally in low gear even on level roads. Still, it was so exhausting that I decided to splurge on a hotel room when I reached Hillsboro, New Mexico.

"What's the price of a single?" I asked the silver-haired lady manager.

"Well, it's a big room with a splendid view and a private bath."

"How much, please?"

"And it's very warm and has clean sheets and towels . . ."

"Fine, fine, but I must know the price."

"Would . . . would two dollars be too much?"

"Two dollars!" After that long buildup I expected a quote of $20 or so, but management read my surprise the wrong way.

"Okay, okay. You can have it for one dollar."

The lobby of that hotel was a virtual museum of the old West. In the mind's eye I could see them still, a hefty mama pounding out honky-tonk tunes on the piano, poker games around tables in the corner, a painted woman of leisure invitingly leaning over the balcony, horses tied just outside, a quarrel at the long bar erupting into six-gun violence. For me, for that one night, at least, the price of a room hadn't inflated much since that bygone era.

This side of Emory Pass smudge pots burned in orchards to fend off a killing frost. A long ride up the flank of the Black Range of the Rockies was almost—almost—as exciting as the trip down the far side. Maybe it was the high thin air blotting out my reason. Or maybe it was the small boy in me looking down from a bicycle at 8,000 feet for the first time. Whatever it was, I decided to coast all the way down without using my brakes.

Fortunately, the road was wide and free of traffic, else I might not be sitting at a typewriter now. It was a wild ride, wild and savage, jerking through hairpin turns at thirty-five miles an hour instead of the ten miles per hour posted on warning signs, riding high at one curve, cutting thin on another, leaning just enough each time, a wind hurrying me along, the wheels singing, down, down, down. And getting safely to the bottom.

After I pedaled out of Silver City I started thinking of the rigors of the forthcoming climb up to the top of the Continental Divide. Like a football coach imploring the impressionable young men under his command to greater fury, I gave myself an inflammatory pep talk, not the least of it a reminder that I had to scale the Divide for the sake of my own booming pride. After all that psychological warfare the climb was a piece of cake, easy and relaxed, the whole thing consuming no more than a few minutes.

In Arizona I rode hard all one lonely day in the reasonable expectation that I would catch up with a hot three-course meal that evening. The town of Guthrie looked promising. It had an airport and a drive-in theater. Guthrie had an airport and a drive-in theater all right but no restaurant, no cafe, not even a grocery store. Some Mexican kids who sold me bean-and-meat burritos were convulsed when the food brought tears to my eyes. Well, I'd been looking forward to a good hot meal.

"Don't you go sleeping out at night," an old-timer in Guthrie warned me.

"Why not?" I put the question to be sociable.

"There's rattlesnakes, gila monsters and stinging scorpions out there."

"So I've heard." I'd heard it endlessly, of course. "But I've been sleeping out for weeks now and haven't seen one yet."

"Yeah, but you ain't been in Arizona yet before."

I spun 142 enervating miles and made a campsite near Florence Junction, Arizona shortly after dark. To be on the safe side I pushed the bike through soft sand for 100 yards or so, pitched my tent in a clearing beyond some stately cactus. After a long day such as that I fell asleep like a log.

A shout awakened me in the middle of the night. Gears clashed, and a car moved along the roadway not far from my hiding hole. The car stopped, moved slowly forward, stopped again. It was obvious the driver was in search of something. Question: Was he in search of me?

The car speeded on ahead, stopped, turned around. It returned to exactly the spot where the bike had left its tracks in the sand. Out they came, five of them, five voices, one of them feminine, shouting and cursing, hell-bent on violence, following the tracks, ominously moving through the night.

I thought of the handgun a friend of my brother suggested I carry. I thought of a club, a sprint deeper into the brush, a quick puncture of a high-pressure tire, which might sound like a gun. But that would reveal my position. I'm not big and muscular, far from it, and odds of five to one were too great.

For a long moment I thought the episode was a fantasy, a smoke ring, the edge of a bad dream. But as the interlopers drunkenly followed the tell-tale tracks leading to my camp their loud, rackety dialogue confirmed my most despairing suspicions.

"Do you really think we ought to do this on Sunday?"

"Who's got the knife?"

"Let me have a part in the fun."

"How can you see"—my belly churned on hearing this—"to aim that thing in the dark?"

They were only twenty feet away now, and coming all too fast. Suddenly the man in the lead gave a blood-curdling scream. The scream lifted, enlarged, filled the night. He had fallen into a barrel cactus, the long needle-sharp thorns had jabbed deep in his face and neck. The wail of pain was so great I nearly felt sorry for him. One slight misstep on his part cancelled out whatever horrors they were to inflict on me. Off they went, back to the road, into the car, the long scream still cutting.

Early next morning I followed a trail of blood to the main road, pedaled easily to Phoenix, where I stayed with friends for two weeks. During my stay I gave several lectures on computer art, which helped replenish my dwindling cash flow situation. The more I talked of my bicycle tour around the house, the more curious my host Mic Lowther became.

"Why can some people like you take off on an extended trip and seem to get so much out of life," he softly asked one evening, "while a hard-working person like me is stuck in a big city office all his life? It doesn't seem right."

"I simply decided that I'd enjoy taking my retirement now and work when I'm too old to enjoy rigorous travel," I said, choosing my words. "You obviously enjoy the challenge of your job, the comforts of your home and the love of your family."

Yet I could see a burgeoning wanderlust begin to warm. Months later, Mic wrote me a letter brimming with enthusiasm. He was taking a seven-month leave of absence from his job so he, his wife and their eleven-year-old daughter could walk the entire Appalachian Trail.

In Flagstaff I found more generous hospitality, more paid lectures, more sightsee side trips. I rode the bike to 9,600 feet on Humphrey's Peak, the highest in Arizona, and crossed 89 miles without a facility en route to the Grand Canyon. Carrying a borrowed backpack, I hiked down to the floor of the Canyon and slept the night.

At Lee's Ferry I asked the Canyoneers if I could work my way on a raft trip through the Canyon. I offered to cook, wash dishes, make camp, gather wood in exchange for a free ride.

"No, sorry," the head boatman said. "But it is kind of neat, you riding a bike around the world. Why don't you join us as a non-paying guest."

Down we went, shooting the Colorado River, high stone walls rising on either side, bighorn sheep occasionally silhouetted against the sky, a trip I'll always remember because I can't ever forget. The bike, the

traffic, the desert and the earth in general faded as we floated down
the big boiling river. Clear blue skies stretched over us every day, stars
and a slitted moon filled the night. Below waterfalls I soaked in the
sunshine, unwinding from the grind of the bike, feeling the cold water
rinse my body, refresh my spirit. The world out beyond the rim of the
canyons seemed fuzzy and far away—and I was contented.

After my time on the river it was difficult to adjust to the clamorous
beat of the road. I pedaled into a hard wind, fought with heavy traffic
for a sliver of highway. Numb, soaked with sweat, my focus a bit
blurred, I checked into a motel on the edge of Kingman and rested up
for what lay ahead.

What lay on the far side of Las Vegas was Death Valley, mean
country, especially for a stranger riding a bike. At a country store I
bought a cold drink from a twinkling gray-haired lady, who asked if
I knew just where I was.

"Somewhere in Nevada, I think."

"Yeah, but what county," she asked.

"You've got me there."

"Mister, you're in Nye County, Nye County, Nevada, the only place
in the United States where prostitution is perfectly legal."

She was still beaming as I rode away toward the blank territory
people had warned me to avoid. To hear these well-meaning people
tell it, Death Valley was a high-risk trip I ought not try, with the
sizzling temperatures dropping below 100 degrees only at night. Maybe
so. But from high on the eastern ridge, the air was cool, the valley
looked fairly promising.

But once I rolled down into Death Valley the heat hit me like a
furnace. Halfway down, the asphalt was melting and glued to the tires.
At the very bottom the thermometer read a hellish 107 degrees with
no wind. Loaded with six quarts of water, remembering the old touchstone about a trip of 1,000 miles beginning with a single step, I crossed
the floor of the valley and then started pumping up a track laddering
5,000 feet in the next 17 miles.

I rode until long after dark. Muscles straining, sweat salting my face,
I rode until I could go on no more. I slept in the desert for a few hours,
pushed on long before dawn. When the sun lighted the fire in this natural oven my lungs began to burn, my back ached, my eyes glazed
over again. I was riding in low gear, riding with what little vitality I
could muster.

Slowly, at a pace of four miles an hour on the steepest hills, I climbed out of the clutches of Death Valley. At eight o'clock I triumphantly collapsed on Townes Pass, my most difficult challenge behind me. But satisfaction didn't last for long. The road dropped into Panamint Valley and then climbed for another twelve steep, sweltering miles. At the risk of sun stroke or heat exhaustion I rode all day despite the heat and the brutal grade.

From the top of a second pass the road runs across a high barren plateau. No fences, no power lines, no buildings, little vegetation intrude on the empty land.

In the midst of that ride across the high country I heard the grind of a car behind me. Motorists frequently stopped for a chitchat, of course, but they stopped somewhere in front of me. A vile nightmare flickered. There I am, all by myself, cycling a lonely road on the edge of nowhere, when a carload of mouth-breathers rough me up, dump me in a remote canyon, steal my money, camera, bike and other belongings.

I looked out of the tail of my eye, saw an arm appear from the window of the car close behind me. Hoping another car would wind up the road, if only for company, I put on a little speed and wondered when the blow might come. But nothing happened. I turned, turned completely around, saw the arm was waving a can of Budweiser.

"You looked like you needed this," a brawny man in a blue VW said, handing the beer over, before he sped away.

In California I took a day off to climb to the top of Mount Whitney, elevation 14,494 feet. It was a good climb, hard and strenuous, challenging without any real perils, and I realized how much mountainclimbing meant to me. If there was any possible way of arranging it, I wanted a shot at the big one, Mount McKinley, in Alaska, although chances for such an ambitious detour were probably remote.

After that climb up Whitney, after I mounted Maria again, the road stretched straight as an arrow, fairly wide, without so much as a whisper of traffic to it. The situation cried out for a flat-out sprint. I lined the bike up on the center line, bent my body like a ski jumper in flight and let go. The speedometer panned to 60 on the long downgrade. I had a feeling the bike and I might actually have taken off if it weren't for the heavy saddlebags.

By lunchtime I was in Benton, 108 miles away. I fought a strong west wind further on, had to walk the bike some in the thin biting air, up into Tioga Pass. I made my way slowly before camping beside a great drift of snow, and covered the remainder of it in cold but less windy weather the next morning. Two days later the road was shut down because of heavy snow.

At the Crane Flat campgrounds a rackety crash awakened me in the night. A bear, no doubt about it, a bloody marauding bear. Unfortunately I had my food beside me in the tent, which meant the bear would snuffle right inside following the scent. But this particular bear must have had a head cold. While he demolished garbage cans on all sides, he left the bonanza inside the tent untouched.

In Yosemite the waterfalls thundered straight off the picture post-cards, the hard granite walls of El Capitan glistened in the shine of morning light. But four spokes broke in Yosemite, and I had to mend a flat on a spectacular run along the Merced River. A total of ten spokes, all of them on the freewheel side of the rear wheel, broke before

Maria and Lloyd enjoying the beauties of Mirror Lake in Yosemite National Park, California

Arrival at the Pacific Ocean, south of San Francisco

I pushed the bike in to another Schwinn dealer, who replaced the spokes and trued the crooked wheel.

I accepted a ride with a motorist after being blown off the bike twice by trucks in a high wind. In the Santa Clara Valley I paid seven cents for a breakfast of coffee, two bananas and a pint of cherry tomatoes. I stayed with friends in Los Altos Hills for a week instead of the single night originally planned.

After I left there I pedaled forty miles of city, topped a hump of a hill and focused on a sight I had been seeking for six months. Seagulls soared overhead, the Pacific Ocean rolled up into a sandy beach. It may sound silly, but I had a catch in my throat. The first significant leg of my journey was completed. Whatever lay ahead, even if I got no further, I had ridden a bike across the United States, which, as my friend John said when I first started, would be quite a feat, if only I could bring it off.

At that point the logical, reasonable, rational thing to do would be to leave immediately for Hawaii, right. So I phoned a friend in Anchorage and asked whether a traverse expedition over Mount McKinley was scheduled. It was. I was invited to join if I could get to Alaska in the next month.

I pushed on north on what was becoming a badly damaged bike. With spokes breaking like toothpicks, the back wheel became so warped that it was often simpler to push the bike. In Eureka, California I had the whole back wheel replaced, which improved my transportation, for a while.

In a leisurely week I reached the top of California and crossed over into Oregon. It was lovely country to travel at a nice pace. Roads were safer and less steep, state parks and views were abundant, seascapes along the way were magnificent. I made 147 miles in one day. I rolled on through Portland and aimed at Mount Hood in the first rain I had experienced since crossing the Mississippi River four months earlier.

At Government Camp I took refuge in a rest shelter. Buster Mann, small and slight, a genial chain-smoking redneck sort who served as custodian, listened attentively while I explained that I planned to spend the night right there in the shelter. His hard eyes squinted almost shut.

"You don't want to sleep here," he said. "Get your bike and follow me."

I followed his red pickup to a snug little cabin he was building himself, warm and dry, furnished with a bed and an easy chair. I awakened to a crackling fire and a breakfast of bacon, eggs, bread, potatoes, beer for Buster, hot jello for me.

Further on, the Lewis and Clark Trail stretched along the Columbia River, washing under the grid of a toll bridge. Just as I got to cycling at a nice speed on the trail a tire blew. I patched and booted the tire as well as I could. It lasted exactly four miles on the odometer before it blew again. This time I had no choice. Since I was carrying no spare, which I vowed to do in the future, I had to hitch 80 miles to Yakima, Washington for a replacement.

I killed some time in Washington backpacking into Mount Saint Helens in search of signs of Bigfoot, with only busted luck. I explored the San Juan Islands, visited with strangers in sleepy villages and stacked up some sleep. I completed my tour of the American West convinced it had been as fascinating as the American East had been frustrating—but perhaps that was because I'd rolled up enough miles to become more than a tenderfoot.

Then I packed everything I needed and caught a plane north from Seattle. Next stop: Anchorage.

Chapter 3

Alaska

Nothing is quite so much fun as trying to sleep through a summer night in Alaska, except maybe a stiff neck. Unfortunately, the two are not total strangers. If all the stiff necks I suffered turning and tossing, tossing and turning in an attempt to sleep through nights when there was so little darkness were laid end to end, I'd be spending the next year in traction.

For a country boy accustomed to the dusk-to-dawn sleeping cycle, I had to make obvious adjustments in Alaska. Unless I managed to vary a lifelong pattern, there was a risk I would get practically no sleep at all. Along with the psychological challenge of bedding down while it was still light enough to read a book outside, the country I was cycling through south from Anchorage was buzzing with something I thought I had left behind—mosquitoes.

Since almost everything in Alaska is bigger than life, I wasn't surprised that the mosquitoes ran to epic dimensions, too. It wasn't long before I learned why. They fed very well. Certainly they fed well on me. A friend told me that a wedge of mosquitoes can drain enough blood out of a naked man in two minutes to run him straight to the nearest hospital.

My friend Margaret, an attractive girl, whom I nicknamed Little Red Wing, tough and effervescent, with dark auburn hair she wore in twin ponytails, rode a bike alongside me. After a few days I realized that I had better keep our relationship in proper focus unless I wanted to jeopardize the rest of my global trip. But every once in a while I thought about settling down to homestead a spread of land in Alaska with her.

We looped the Turnagain Arm, saw the big icebergs on Portage Lake, spotted a few Dall sheep high on the mountainside. Sometimes parts of Alaska were surprisingly similar to the Florida Everglades. Grassy swampland was studded with conifers and stretched for miles.

"Where you come from?" a bearded old sourdough dressed like a tramp waved us down one day.

"America—I mean Virginia, Charlottesville, Virginia," I replied.

"Good for you. How about a soda pop? And some smoked salmon?"

It sounded too good to resist. It tasted too good, as well, salmon just out of the smoker, juicy, tender, with a flavor like nothing I can remember. The sourdough in the baggy clothes turned out to be an elementary school principal, and he insisted we join him for a dinner of roast moose and morel mushrooms. If the world was beginning to widen for me, so was the attendant bill of fare.

In Homer Little Red Wing and I ordered up banana splits—for all the exotic new tastes, I hadn't lost my appetite for three-star banana splits—by way of celebrating 250 miles on the road. In and around Kachemak Bay we helped two families lift the beams for their new log cabins, rode a sailboat through a bright cone of water to watch seals sunning on a far rock.

Now that I felt I knew the country some we hooked a ride back to Anchorage. But we didn't stay for long. I was eager to get to Talkeetna to check my climbing gear, camp within sight of the mountain and work myself into the proper emotional pitch for the ascent. We rode a bus to the end of the line and set out in heavy, untracked wilderness, with Mount McKinley, its flanks covered with snow, rising into misty skies to the south.

We swam a clear lake, walked savage land, swam in a river we hadn't planned to swim until we fell in. After setting our course by the shadows of the trees we finally reached Wonder Lake and caught the last bus to Talkeetna. When it came time to part I found it difficult to say good-bye to Margaret/Little Red Wing. We had been part of one another's lives, if only for a little while, and although those were days and nights to remember, they were days and nights to be missed, too.

On joining the others scheduled for the climb, I heard the bad news. Three members of a five-woman party from Japan had gone up for the summit from a high camp two weeks earlier and never returned. A petite mountain-tanned woman named Sekita, who shared camping rights with me in bush pilot Don Sheldon's hangar, desperately clung

to the frail hope they might somehow still be alive. Fatigued, worn
with worry, she badgered the pilot for information, jumped any time
the phone rang. Apart from her great concern for companions she had
climbed with before, the Japanese government had cabled to tell her
she couldn't return without the three missing bodies.

"The reason we are here is to do a good job and try to help others,"
the bush pilot told her one night. "You are doing all you can and so
am I. Try to get some sleep and we'll see if we can fly the mountain
again tomorrow."

But Sekita didn't sleep much. Neither did I.

In the mountains hard weather is one of the worst of the killers.
Fifteen thousand square miles of snow and ice around Mount McKinley, or Denali, as they call it in Alaska, can generate its own weather,
which helps explain why only one out of every three parties successfully reaches the summit. As a joke, I told the others weather would
be the least of our worries simply because I was part of the team. After
all, I'd had only four days of rain in eight months of cycling across the
country from Virginia.

The pilot flew the twelve of us to the southern Kahiltna Glacier. A
silent world, blindingly bright and overwhelming, rose over us. We
tied on our snowshoes, clipped into the ropes and shouldered eighty-
pound life support systems. We climbed slowly for two hours before
we left the packs in a sheltered area. Then we climbed back down the
glacier for another heavy load. Twenty days on a mountain call for
an abundance of food and camping gear.

Twenty days on a mountain calls for every conceivable safety pre-
caution, too. We did most of our climbing at night, for example, and
rested when the snow bridges were soft in the heat of the day. After
we reached the end of the glacier we exchanged cumbersome snowshoes for crampons.

One afternoon I awakened from a wooly nap to tighten a tent support. Suddenly, the snow disappeared beneath me. I heard snow
softened by sun crash for hundreds of feet down below. Wedged in
under my armpits, dangling precariously as a rag doll, my feet reached
for footing without finding anything. I couldn't even shout for fear
the noise might break my tentative hold. Finally someone saw me and
passed a snowshoe to help pull me out. But I'd experienced the dangers
of the mountain for a few bad moments.

The higher we climbed, the more spectacular the views became.
The weather was perfect, bright and sunny by day, with the sun so hot
against the snow that it burned any unprotected flesh. Somehow even

the tip of my tongue got burned while we cautiously moved up the highest mountain in all America.

At 14,000 feet we all of us had a jolt. Three specks of color intruded on the white surface higher up. Naturally we offered to delay our own climb and see if these specks were the missing Japanese climbers. Sekita, the leader of the Japanese women, and Jiro, a thick, muscular husband of one of the missing girls, flew in to assist.

We skinned up the mountain for another two hours before we knew for sure. The specks of color became clothes, the lengths became bodies. Sekita and Jiro hesitated going forward. In the end the husband broke down, of course, although he must have realized that at least his wife, an accomplished climber who loved the mountains, had died embarked on a challenge she loved. And on the basis of a post-mortem, they had died quickly by falling, probably some 3,000 feet, instead of slowly freezing or starving.

Over a period of many years I have spent considerable time up in the bittersweet mountain world. I've climbed them, camped in the thin air, even had an occasional minor accident of my own. Yet this was the first time I had seen death close-up in the higher altitudes I loved so much. It wasn't pretty, far from it, it wasn't easy to bear. Yet it was a built-in peril everyone who clamps on boots recognizes without quite articulating in crowds, and this dreadful incident merely confirmed the bleak realities.

We moved the bodies. We moved the stiff frozen bodies as carefully as we could down the steep face of Mount McKinley. We moved them down to the basin at 14,000 feet, where the bush pilot could land and fly them out. Before the plane arrived, Sekita and Jiro had a small religious ceremony with an incense candle and thanked us for our understanding.

Months later, a friend asked if the experience didn't diminish our own enthusiasm for the climb. It didn't. But it did enlarge our respect for the power of the mountain.

Next day we awakened to the only heavy snow we encountered through the climb. It was a hard push to make it to the edge of the steepest slope of them all. We used crampons and ice axes, climbing with infinite caution, remembering those three bright specks in the snow. When we reached that last malevolent slope we paused and adjusted our loads again.

I stood beneath a near vertical ice slope peering up, up, up to where it disappeared in clouds when it happened. It happened all of a sudden, just like that. The snow moved in a powerful lurch. Directly above me a whiplash sounded, and then a great rumbling noise. The alarming sights and sounds spelled out what was so plainly unfolding: Avalanche!

I went absolutely stiff. I screamed, screamed again, a long wail blotted out by the thunderous crack of the avalanche. Helpless, a terrible singing in my ears, still absolutely stiff with fear, I begged my body to react by jumping, coiling up, running, something. But I remained right there, numb, until the mountain hit. It bowled me over, tumbling me through the snow, pinwheeling me down the slope, a piddling sack of clothes helplessly pinned in the elements. It looked very much as if Mount McKinley had claimed another intruder so bold as to test it.

Yet my arms instinctively fanned out in an attempt to stop the roll. They clawed desperately at the snow, clawed for some sort of tentative hand-hold. I still don't know quite how it happened, and, now that I look back on it, I don't much care, but they grabbed onto a jagged edge of ice, held, braked me while the avalanche rolled on down. I was still scared stiff, exhausted right down to the bones, but I had survived.

After an escape like that we prudently decided to descend to our last camp and await safer conditions. Stiff and sore, we lit a campstove to boil some tea. We napped some, had a high-protein dinner, slept a long night before it was time to climb again.

Moving up the near vertical slope of the West Buttress, we pulled over a few inches of snow covering blue ice. Our eighty-pound loads lay like iron on our backs, our bodies throbbed with fatigue. In the thin air almost three miles high we pulled for more oxygen. It was a day to remember, a day to forget.

Rolled in my bag that night, the mute mountain all round me, I filed a cryptic entry in my notebook: "Anyone fortunate enough to view this scene would never again wonder why men climb mountains."

We went up the narrow buttress next day, using ropes and crampons whenever we had to, up to where we could look down another 3,000 feet on one side and almost as far on the other. We couldn't help but think of the dead Japanese girls here. This was no place to slip.

We left our next camp at an elevation of 17,300 feet in bright, glittery sunshine. We were reaching for the summit now, reaching hard, almost on schedule. We slanted up sheets of steep ice to Denali Pass, abandoned most of our packs. With the summit visibly within our sights, unless something went badly wrong, we climbed with more determination than energy as the heights squeezed at our lungs.

"Walking with the angels" at 16,300 feet on Mount McKinley, Alaska

When the group I was tied to fell behind others in the party, I was invited to unrope and go on ahead. For a long venturesome distance I climbed all by myself. As a loner by nature, I generally find it difficult to climb in company and at someone else's pace. I felt a sense of heady exultation, of oneness with nature, just the two of us there, Mount McKinley and me, with every cautious booted step carrying me closer toward the summit.

Further up, the burden was almost unbearable. It took four deep breaths to fuel a single step, a longer rest every forty steps. But the lure of the summit wiped out some of the agony. We were driven

Climbing on the West Buttress at 17,000 feet on Mount McKinley. Mount Foraker is in the background.

climbers, consumed by the spectacle so close above us, reaching only for the top. It isn't surprising that mountaineers often die in summit storms. A diminished mental capacity at high altitudes and an understandable impatience to reach the crest can blur the vital judgment factor.

On the last ridge I peered 8,000 feet straight down, a dizzying triumphant sight. But the slightly higher rise up ahead riveted me. I paused thirty feet short of the top, now whispering close to my most vaulting dream, in an effort to get a grip on my emotions. Finally I climbed those last few feet. There I stood, finally, at the very top of McKinley, up on the highest point in all North America, savoring the satisfaction without even speaking.

But we had little time for any celebrations. Some members of the team had pushed themselves beyond their physical limits. One man was almost delirious, with no sense of direction, which meant I had to act as anchor man on the steep descent. Our assistant leader had pneumonia, and pulmonary edema made it impossible for him to

The author on the summit of Mount McKinley, 20,320 feet

survive in that thin air for long. We rigged a sled to get him down to 15,000 feet, where he could be evacuated by helicopter. With our loads too heavy, we decided to carry food for only three days, which wasn't enough, as we realized five days later.

Although none of us had ever seen the far side of McKinley before, we made a traverse of the mountain. After a day and a half of tough traveling down Harpers Glacier, a chopper came in for our ailing companion. One at a time, on a tight relay, we moved on down the knife edge of Karsten's Ridge, the single most dangerous stage of the whole climb. When we had to stop for sleep, we were forced to chip a platform on the narrow ridge.

Toward the bottom of the ridge we prayed our good luck with the weather would somehow last another day. After all, we couldn't possibly descend in a storm. We were nearly out of food now, nearly out of vitality. In Denali Pass, where other climbers have recorded winds of 140 miles an hour and temperatures of minus—repeat: minus—fifty degrees, it was clear and warm, with only a mild breeze.

A miracle? In my view the surprisingly bland weather and lack of high-velocity wind was due to the healing powers of what I came to call Loga, for Lloyd's Own Guardian Angel. The skeptical reader might well wonder whether Loga actually contributed. I admit to not being convinced myself when I began my trip. But strange happenings went beyond the limits of coincidence, beyond the edge of luck, beyond any other explanation I could find, not only up on Denali Pass but elsewhere in my subsequent travels. By the time my long ride was over and done with two years hence I knew that Loga was the real thing.

In perfect weather we slogged down the Muldrow Glacier to McGonagal Pass. Who could blame me for kissing a dwarf fireweed flower in the pass? It was the first plant life I'd seen in more than two weeks. The lovely clear weather held as we moved along a tundra flickering with mosquitoes, forded the wide, wide McKinley River and climbed three numbing miles to reach the park road.

At last we were down, all the way down, our triumph behind us, dirty, scruffy, smelly, tired, ravenous. We wolfed down our first food in two days, eating like millhands, tearing at the meat. We talked, talked round a campfire far into the night. We had a lasting bond now, all of us. We had spent 17 days going more than 100 miles up Mount McKinley and back down.

I resisted a scratchy impulse to cycle the Alaska Highway. It would have been pleasant if I'd had the vigor and the money drained away

At the Seattle airport, wearing and carrying everything necessary for a bicycle trip around the world

for the climb. But I returned to Seattle to pick up the pieces of my west-ward ho tour of the world by truck, by train and by ferryboat.

In Seattle I took two months off to restore my funds and energy. Along with resting up and eating fairly regularly again, I gave a series of lectures and slide shows on computer art and wrote some travel articles for a newspaper back home. My economic situation improved considerably, not enough to put me into any middle or upper brackets, mind you, which seem beyond my limits, but enough to start making plans for my departure.

The bike got a brand-new rim, heavier, hopefully stronger, as well. For the sake of trimming bulk and weight I exchanged my two-man tent for a single, my four-pound sleeping bag for an equally warm two-pounder. I wheedled the shipping people until I found that even ordinary cruise ships cost more than air fare. In the end I beat the system by buying a one-way ticket to Sydney, with free stopovers in San Francisco, Hawaii and Auckland, if I chose to trigger them.

Once I got my blood up, there was no stopping me. I wanted to beat the system a second time, especially with excess baggage costing ap-proximately as much as raw gold. I knew the weight of the bicycle, my gear and clothes would run well beyond the forty-four-pound inter-national limit. So I wore all my clothes, three layers of them, one on top of the other, stuffed my pockets with camera lenses, repair tools, flashlights and waddled in to the Pan American departure counter in Seattle.

An attendant behind the desk slowly looked me up and down. He nodded, nodded and smiled, familiar with a ruse he obviously had seen many times before.

"I hate to be the one to tell you this, sir," he said, the smile lingering on his face. "But Hawaii is a domestic flight, you know—not interna-tional. You can carry all the weight you want."

I felt a fool. I'd felt a fool before, and I'd feel a fool many times again. But I felt a particular fool wearing three layers of clothes, my pockets bulging with gear, in the heat of a pleasant day.

We stopped off briefly at San Francisco, flew high over the Pacific for Hilo. I did the best I could trying to shift gears for strange sights, strange customs, strange people. With the world trip unwinding again, I was passing the point of no return.

Chapter 4

Hawaii

There it was, barely visible through the window of the airplane, tiny, no more than a flyspeck at first, gradually enlarging until I could see enough of it to know without the captain's mechanical in-flight commentary, the dark lava coast washed with foam, the verdant interior, occasional small huts sheltered by coconut palms. Aloha!

The wheels of the jet got a firm grip, the wing flaps fanned out to help brake our rush along the landing strip. A flicker of excitement stirred as we unloaded at General Lyman Field in Hilo. The fact that I had reached Hawaii filled in another yearning old daydream.

No hula dancer wearing little more than a grass skirt greeted me with a lei of orchids, no string band raised a welcoming din, no grand hotel with smiling tourists lifting long cool drinks on the terrace appeared. But if my first exposure to Hawaii didn't measure up to the hyperbole of the travel folders, I had no complaints. Under a thin cloud cover the air was warm, warm and sweet.

It was so warm, in fact, that I treated myself to a brief nap on an unyielding ridge of lava near the airport. Spinning up a back road, rejoicing to have crossed still another personal frontier, I encountered a surprising number of people, all of them warm and friendly. The honey-sweet scent of the flowers, the picture postcard palms, the great ball of sun riding up the rim of the sky all contributed to my contentment.

But I had miles to go and an old promise to keep. More than anything else, I wanted to scale Mauna Kea, Hawaii's highest peak, 13,796
feet—the figures twirled in my head—above sea level, its summit
frosted with snow. I learned that an essential camping permit as well
as a clearance for the climb could be had in Hilo.

Hilo is a small rural town with a bizarre claim to fame. It's the only
city in the United States whose grid of dikes protects it not from flood
waters but from lava flows. Nobody ever saved the town by sticking
a finger in that dike. Hilo also thrums with practicing skeptics convinced that an inbound tourist ought to show a little respect.

"You plan to bicycle over the Saddle Road to Mauna Kea? Don't.
It's been done only once before."

"You're out of your mind . . ."

"Saddle Road? Even in a jeep it's very tough."

And so it was. Saddle Road rises 6,500 feet fairly fast, an endless
track, the surface pocked with deep chuckholes, which give it the look
of a lunar landscape. Sweating hard, the sting of salt burning my eyes,
pausing every so often because I couldn't see, I rode the winding slope
past clusters of wild orchids without seeing those ritual symptoms of
civilization, houses and power lines. I saw no grocery stores, either,
which made me wonder whether I had food enough for the climb.

Once I left the Saddle Road, I pumped for three miles up a sand
and gravel road, a bit better, or not quite as bad, at least until it rose
more than 10 percent and cost me any real traction. Like it or not, I
had no choice. I hid Maria in a convenient crater, stuffed the sleeping
bag, the tent and what little food I had into my pack, and set out afoot.

A can of cold beans hardly amounted to a three-star dinner, especially after a long day on the road, but it was better than no dinner at
all. Besides, the strain of the flight, the brief sightsee and the preliminary ascent had let the air out of my vitality. I fell asleep almost as soon
as I squeezed into the sleeping bag.

Hours before dawn, I awakened to see two huge red spots burn a
hole in the dark sky off to my right. They were big, both of them, big
as forest fires, enormous balls of color, identity unknown until,
abruptly, I identified them as Mauna Ulu and Alae, Hawaii's two
active volcanoes, which I vowed to visit first chance I had. Like that
jiffy dinner the night before, my breakfast wasn't all it might have
been: a candy bar.

Then up I went, climbing fairly fast, reaching for sure footholds in
the cinder, rocks and lava flows, the vegetation all below me now, up,
up, up self-propelled to 12,000 vertical feet in just 24 hours. But eventually I made it to the top, which was cold and windy, the highest peak

in Hawaii, the highest peak on earth if the height is reckoned from its base 20,000 feet below sea level. "Mother Earth," I told myself, "that was one resounding belch."

As a general rule going down a mountain is faster than going up. After I retrieved Maria and locked my feet onto the pedals again, it was faster still, almost too fast there a couple of times, the road descending at such an angle that I actually passed a car at a speed of sixty miles per hour. The driver, blinking in disbelief, gave me a friendly honk as I whooshed by. I flattened in a streamlined position to twine through the next twist of curves without losing any speed.

Predictably, I was so exhausted, so dirty and so hungry that I didn't know exactly which luxury to indulge in first when I signed into a hotel in a resort town named Kailua. In the end, I opted for that standard American bill of fare, a T-bone steak, before a long bath and an even longer sleep. After all, a total intake of two candy bars and six cookies during the long day hadn't put nearly enough fuel in the engine.

South of Hookeena a rutted road crosses several layers of lava still bulging from the 1950 eruption of Mauna Loa. Residents have some cause to talk wonderingly of that eventful blast. The eruption went on and on, twenty-three days in all, yielding an epic river of lava, enough to pave a four-lane highway more than four times around the world.

In view of the 1950 eruption, my feelings were mingled cycling through the Hawaii Volcanoes National Park. The prospect of actually seeing a volcano close-up stirred me. On the other hand, I wasn't especially reassured on hearing that the observation platform built over the rim had collapsed in the crater, although a new one already underway might be completed and opened the next day for traffic, if the winds were from the northeast.

As things turned out, they were. I piled out of the tent, dressed quickly, gulped an instant breakfast. After a long impatient wait at park headquarters I climbed on Maria and we went spinning, spinning down the trail along the Chain of Craters Road. I overtook the standard little old ladies in tennis shoes, more youthful ladies in heels and long-haired young men wearing sandals, all of them walking across sharp lava, all of them bound for a look at Mauna Ulu.

Hurrying, pushing past others after I abandoned the bike, I reached the crater rim and looked down into a classic vision of Hell. Lava, a whole lake of lava, bubbled up out of the lower depths, churning, rumbling, smoking, a heaving black mass streaked with liquid yellows and exploding into great balls, a sight to catch at the breath. I gasped, overwhelmed by the sight and sound of it.

"Back, back, we have to go back!" A park ranger raised his voice another notch. "The winds are changing, the fumes can kill you."

The ranger was in no way exaggerating. He'd done time at the park for several years. He was aware of the hazards. Yet somehow I wasn't able to turn and leave. Thick coils of sulphur rose out of the crater, sour, half-choking me, and the ranger yelled to clear the area again. I snapped pictures as long as I could, more pictures than I had film for, and then I snapped imaginary pictures strictly for the memory, click-click, until it was possible to stay no longer. On the way out I put some substance to those assorted pictures by collecting strands of stringy volcanic discharge and tear-shaped grits of lava falling around us.

"Lloyd? Lloyd Sumner?" A twenty-one-gun smile of recognition lighted his wide, blue-eyed face. "What in the world are you doing out here?"

Halfway up a hill on the way to Akaka Falls a car had pulled to a stop as I went wheeling toward the top. Out of the front seat came Ross Newton, rump-sprung as ever, a big gregarious fellow itinerant I had first met during his hitchhike near Death Valley and then again on my return from Alaska, when he insisted on fixing me an extra cup of tea at the Prince Rupert ferryboat. This time he insisted I spend a few days at his dairy farm.

The experience was a pleasant blur, good company and stimulating conversation, new sights to be seen, coffee growing in the wild, mongoose, wild pigs, life at a fundamental level. When I asked Ross where I might replenish my tattered wardrobe at bargain basement prices, he led me to exactly the right outlet. Two pair of long pants, two aloha shirts and a bathing suit came to a total—a *total*, mind you—of $1.05.

During my time with Ross Newton, during my time in Hawaii generally, I found economics to be pretty much what you want to make of them. A coke costs $.25, for example; a can of pineapple juice the identical size costs $.11. On my hairline budget, I developed a prodigious thirst for pineapple juice.

On a hike through Waipio Canyon one morning we passed a glistening waterfall so perfect that it might have been painted on the land. The girl stretched on the black sand by the falls might have been painted too, if someone happened to get lucky. For a long moment there I wasn't sure that my vision hadn't gone hazy.

"Ross, did you see what we just passed?"

"Sure. They call it a woman."

"I know. But she didn't have any clothes on."

"Come to think about it, she didn't. How about that!"

A description of that woman in the raw, all pectoral muscles and flowing hair, later caused a friend's whimsical old memory to stir. According to old-timers in radio, an announcer newly hired to do spot commercials somewhere in Minnesota was drilled over and over again before being assigned an especially hazardous job for a local bakery. For obvious reasons, he went through exhaustive drills to make certain the words didn't run together: ". . . prepared by master (pause) bakers . . . eat Langendorf's and you will have the best in bread."

On the day the novice became air-borne a director seated in the control room tightened up some as the ticklish passage arrived. But the announcer couldn't have performed with more clarity. ". . . prepared by master (long pause) bakers," he intoned without running the words together, whereupon the director and an engineer let out a sigh of relief, ". . . eat Langendorf's and you will have the breast in bed."

Before my stay with Newton came to an end he enticed me into a morning of skin diving, an exciting prospect despite the fact I had never tried the sport. I wasn't apprehensive, not really, not with even kids strapping on a face mask and submerging wherever people gather to get wet, but I wasn't sanguine, either. Along with other assorted defects, I don't happen to be an especially good swimmer, to say the least.

Still, the sensation of skinning out into the Pacific wearing fins, a mask and snorkel was exhilarating. The mask provided a scope into a misty world I hadn't ever seen. Colorful fish stirred down in the depths, fish and jagged sea urchins, and if I had some trouble breathing through my mouth after too many years training myself to suck air in and out through my nose, I managed to adjust and keep at it.

Whatever my proficiency, Newton had more faith than I had. After a few minutes in what amounted to beginner's water, he walked me up the coast to a sandless stretch where lava formations edged with coral led down into the sea. I followed him in, working my fins, swimming straight out, carefully avoiding the sharp coral, passing through narrow channels, until he paused and raised a warning whoop.

"Turn around," he cried. "Turn around and make for shore. The currents, they're much too strong."

I flipped round and made for shore, stroking as hard as I could, pulling for safety, alarmed by the shockpower in his voice. But for all my efforts I could see the hazard through my mask: the coral was passing the wrong way. Churning with a heavy tide, lashed by the channel, the current was sweeping me out to the open sea.

Abruptly a jagged black rock rose out of the foam. I grabbed at it with a stiff arm, pushed off, tumbled on the crest of an enormous wave, my head throbbing, literally keelhauled by the sullen riptide. Somehow I kept struggling—and somehow I finally caught hold of some coral.

"Help!" My voice beat against the tumult. "Help, help!"

Just then a malevolent wave tore me off the coral. I planed through the water, pinwheeling on the jagged bottom. Every time I attempted to clear the mask another wave spun me further. After fighting the sea for as long as I could I realized that I could resist no more.

Drained and exhausted, my quest to bicycle around the world not even half completed, I slipped into a relaxed haze, half of it resignation of what was to come, half in hopes I might gather strength. When I abandoned any realistic hopes, when I felt there was no need to struggle further, a brute of a wave smashed in from my right and lifted me onto a rock shelf. I grabbed, grabbed again, flattened my body on the rim of the sea.

Blood oozed out of a deep cut in my heel; my back was welted with rips from the coral. I watched Ross Newton, reeling, hunched over after his own efforts, scramble to safety fifty yards down the shore. For almost an hour I lay there staring at the sea wondering whether I would ever test it again with a mask and pipe. Probably not, I decided.

A visitor's concept of Hawaii is apt to be highly subjective. Some tourists see it as a golfer's paradise, others as a romantic arena wired with ukuleles, moonlight and dancing girls, still others as an unhurried land where they can unwind and mend the pressures of some great urban grid they have abandoned for a few precious days.

In my opinion Hawaii was all those things—and something more, too. It also amounts to a live green grocery where guavas and mangoes, breadfruit and bananas, raspberries and papaya can be had for the picking. Quite apart from my hairline solvency, a condition those free groceries helped keep afloat, I actually enjoyed living off the land in the manner of our grandparents and great-grandparents.

Cycling toward Seven Sacred Pools, I stepped up my connection with nature. I boiled breadfruit until it tasted like baked potatoes, gorged myself with passion fruit, sucked the juice from the sweetest oranges I ever tasted. While I didn't plan to go into hibernation, I was laying on some fat to sustain me for the unknown track through the country that lay ahead.

One evening I bundled into my sleeping bag after feeding on more than my usual share of wild mangoes. Unaccountably I awakened early, very early, long before dawn—perhaps I was dyspeptic—to

Kalapana Black Sands Beach, Hawaii

find the hills touched by a bright wash of moonlight. The elements were too tempting to resist. Hurriedly dressing, I wheeled Maria through the moonlight, waves whispering from an unseen shore, waterfalls foaming down steep valleys, banana trees arched overhead, a brooding mountain rising above everything, the whole of it almost a spiritual experience.

Another time I thought the menu to be had there in the wild might be enlarged to include some protein. But the wild goats perched on the crags probably were as tough and bristly as they looked and I remained a vegetarian.

NaPali Coast on the island of Kauai, Hawaii

Every once in a while my faith in virtually anything that grows almost did me in. During a rest stop in a shelter of trees near Kalalau Valley I found some nuts, kukui nuts, as I was to learn, smallish, with solid meat centers, a cross between macadamia nuts and coconuts on the basis of a sample taste. Pleased, I sprawled on the ground and began cracking and eating the kukuis, ten, fifteen, twenty, twenty-five or so before I was pleased no more. My lower intestines tied in painful knots, wrung themselves out. Fortunately the tropical vegetation included a profusion of bushes, behind which I emptied myself again and again. I've seldom felt so weak.

"If kukui nuts are properly roasted, they can be eaten in small numbers," an islander told me later. "But if you eat even two or three of them raw you'll get diarrhea. Many more than that, well, a person can get deathly ill."

Still later, two natives expressed great surprise that I was alive after consuming the number I had. Farewell to foraging, I told myself, unless I knew the name, rank and cereal number of exactly what I was eating.

As it happened, I finally arrived at Kalalau on Christmas Day, which seemed as good a time as any, especially when a bearded young man with long alfresco hair stopped me along a trail down into the valley with an invitation for Christmas dinner. The fact that I wore my hair short, was dressed in more traditional garb and, on a relative scale, looked a member of the Establishment in no way diminished the warmth of his invitation.

"You're most welcome to join us," he said. "We're planning a great feast."

Before the stranger departed he gave me precise directions on how to find the cave dwelling where the festivities were to be held. Strolling the beach, a peckish question rose in my mind. If I myself had been dressed in shabby clothes, if I had worn long flowing hair without any real shape to it, would I have been so genuinely welcomed into many homes serving the ritual holiday dinner? The question seemed downright rhetorical.

Early that afternoon semipermanent residents of the valley began to gather at the cave for what the stranger had quite properly described as a feast. They'd been cooking for several days, some of them, in homemade ovens, in kettles, even in a kind of clay fire. The area was neat, brushed and swept, with no litter anywhere in sight.

To work up the proper Christmas spirit, all the guests came dressed in their holiday best, such as it was. One dark-eyed girl wore a colorful maxi skirt, nothing to the north of it. Trader Bill, who'd organized

the arrangements, had vowed to make a complete new outfit for
himself, from head to toe, only he'd run out of time after getting only
as far as a headband and a string of beads, which was all he wore.
Others were equally informal.

My Christmas dinner, circa 1972, began with fruit salad confected
of banana, mango, papaya, oranges, grapefruit and java plum. We
paused, moved on to fresh green watercress, wild rice, coconuts,
memorable mango fritters and turnovers made from poi flour. Instead
of the traditional plum pudding, dessert consisted of large deep-dish
fruit pies, which, if not as evocative, were every bit as good.

Between courses celebrants were invited into the cave for a healing
smoke of marijuana. At the risk of seeming a prude, I passed. I passed
for a brief swim in the ocean. Once I topped up with another round
of that deep-dish pie later, it was time to start moving, with abundant
thanks to the strangers who had kindly treated me to a Christmas with
no humbug to it, to start moving on to New Zealand by way of brief
stopovers in Samoa and Fiji, to ride the rim of the East. Spin, world,
keep spinning. I had no plans to get off.

Chapter 5

New Zealand

New Zealand has a very good press. Everything I had read and heard about the country before my arrival made it sound like a promised land, a territory to explore in a leisurely manner, an arena beyond the usual growing pains. New Zealand lived up to my lofty expectations.

All along I had planned to cycle throughout the country to meet its friendly, outdoors-loving people, see its spectacular fiords, mountains, giant trees, geysers, sandy beaches, volcanoes and wilderness and generally sop up the local flavors. In my travels I would look for the perfect spot where I might want eventually to settle permanently.

This doesn't mean that all the people I encountered in New Zealand were pleasant and friendly. They weren't. Every once in a while I came upon the occasional stiff, antisocial clod with any personality shades rubbed away to the vanishing point.

Will Rogers once said he never met a man he didn't like. Will Rogers never rode a bike toward a windy farmhouse near the Canterbury Plains in search of a retreat for the night. A bulky man appeared, diffident, visibly worn, demonstrating none of the jovial spirits I generally found in New Zealand. He peered at me as if I happened to be a side dish he hadn't ordered.

"Hello." I summoned up all the good cheer I could.

"Humph."

"I'm bicycling around your country, and I can't get any further tonight. Do you mind if I camp on your property, please?"

Resting in one of the many parks in Christchurch, New Zealand

He didn't so much as blink.

"I won't disturb anything." As an old Virginia farmboy, I knew it was tactically wise to change lures when the first offering didn't work. "I don't even carry matches."

He might just as well have been mute.

"I don't need a bed, understand." With the sun slanting down over sloping countryside, I was getting desperate. "All I want is a place to pitch my wee small tent."

"Okay." The farmer spoke, he actually made some noise. "You can sleep in the garage there."

Otherwise the west coast of New Zealand was filled with friendly people and rain. At least I ran into a lot of rain. It came sheeting down, a torrential rain, without stopping for two days and two nights, which got me to wondering whether I shouldn't trade my bicycle in for an ark.

One of many nice people was another farmer, a big brawny man who showed me how he could whistle, grunt or wave his beautiful sheep dogs into performing a variety of specific chores, not the least of them literally running along the backs of the sheep to turn them into another field on the 1,500-acre spread he owned. That same evening his wife showed me a by-product of their farm in the form of a lavish mutton roast, which we finished right down to the bone, and then she insisted on washing my clothes.

Mostly I wandered lonely as a cloud through the west country. I slept wherever I could, ate anything I could lay my hands on, paused to patch a tire any time the hard rutted roads wore a hole in one. I spun up crooked trails, photographed epic waterfalls, climbed mountains with names I hadn't heard before, unwound away from the towns in the enormous sweep of land.

At a tumble-down little village called Okarito, where they probably would roll up the sidewalks at nine o'clock every night, if only they had any sidewalks, the one resident store was shut tight. I had to make do with whatever I could forage for dinner. I made do by gathering a sack of mussels down on the long curve of beach.

Except for the night I got stuck in a primitive shower stall at a hotel in Mossburn I experienced no adversities, not in terms of what still

Riding through the brooding mountains on the west coast of the South Island of New Zealand

lay ahead in other countries. I traveled not only by bike but also afoot, by boat, and by bus; sometimes I rode my thumb, although hitching wasn't as productive in that part of New Zealand as elsewhere. Around Milford Sound I saw literally hundreds of waterfalls foaming down the cliffsides, and explored the windy tunnels of dark caves.

West of Burkes Pass MacKenzie County stretches into an enormous plain, dry and fairly flat, something like the plains in our wheat belt back home in America. I'd bicycled plains before without experiencing any great trouble. But the endless stretch west of Burkes Pass was nothing less than a wind tunnel.

The wind hit me like a wall when the land flattened out. It blew straight through me, cold, an edge of pain to it, relentless, never ceasing. I got an iron grip on the handlebar, tucked my head low as I could, leaned hard into the wind pumping every muscle to advance in my lowest gear. Fortunately, there was little traffic on the open road, and I could use the full width of it to maintain control.

But even so, the wind—I learned later that it was blowing at more than eighty miles an hour—was so strong that I couldn't safely walk the bike after I gave up trying to ride. Howling over the flatland, it bowled me over several times, tangled me in the wheels. Once it actually lifted the front wheel off the pavement when I was attempting to ride again and blew the bike and me off into a hard gravel shoulder. By then I had seen enough of the western rim of New Zealand not to express any surprise when the drivers of a truck and two cars roared with laughter as they passed me by in a distress condition.

The few trees rising on the plain bent double in the swirl of dust and sand, same as I did. Altogether it took me almost three hours to cover a distance of only ten miles on to my next stop at Lake Tekapo. If Will Rogers ever had the chance to visit New Zealand he would have met a wind he didn't like, too.

Soon after I arrived in Auckland the *New Zealand Herald* cornered me for an interview, Yankee Bicycles Around the World, that sort of thing, which was perfectly all right with me, if only because local publicity tends to open an occasional door, warm an occasional friendship. But I had no idea a newspaper feature could lead to where this one seemed to be leading in a lunch room in Ohinewai.

Alison was lovely, blonde and shapely, a knockout of a woman. She had seen my picture in the paper and started a friendly conversation with no real pattern to it. After we talked for a while she smilingly made what sounded like a wildly generous offer.

"If you need a place to sleep in Hamilton, you are welcome to sleep in my bed," she said without a blush.

Stunned, not certain of the folkways in New Zealand after only a few days ashore, my face obviously registered a sense of astonishment fairly high up the scale. She read my face, considered the words she had spoken, amended the offer for the sake of greater clarity.

"Oh, no," she said. "It's in a flat, and I won't be back for a few days."

So much for romance. If that was my first glaring misunderstanding in New Zealand, it was far from my last. After all, I was tuning in to modified English/English. As the days slipped by I became more accustomed to reading signs lettered "Mind That Child," "Slips" and "Greasy if Wet," hearing men address one another as "mate," which I had always interpreted as spouse.

On a hike over the dormant volcano Tongariro I met three fellow spirits from Wellington bound for Mount Ruapehu, elevation 9,150 feet, the highest peak on the north island. Would I care to join them? Of course I would. The climb itself was not especially eventful, although I had to squint to prevent snowblindness without any goggles, but the view from the dome was well worth the trip. We peered down into a spectacular steamy crater lake edged with ice and snow, a vent for the volcano that erupts every few years.

The burly bearded manager of a nearby hotel joined the three of us while we "shouted" each other a few beers following the descent. After hearing a few references to how far I had come on a bicycle, he made a no-nonsense business proposition:

"You show your color slides to my guests one night—and you can stay here free for as long as you like."

Done, and done. I managed to stretch that arrangement out for almost two weeks, which put me far ahead of the game.

During my stay I made a solo climb up the classic cone-shaped volcano Ngauruhoe, tricky, very tricky, dangerous because the ash, pumice and loose sand offered little traction for the last vertical half-mile to the rim. Loose pebbles, rocks and boulders tumbling down the slope threatened to touch off major rockslides; the volcano itself could erupt at any moment. Yet I was so exhausted when I finished the climb that I sat on the rim inhaling sulphur fumes in a cloud of smoke while eating a package lunch.

Before the first week was out I also joined a park guide for a wild ride down the white waters of the Tongariro River. In a lightweight kayak buttoned up at the top, swinging a two-bladed paddle I wasn't all that familiar with, I whooshed the rapids until the river bent

Standing on the edge of hell—the crater of Ngauruhoe volcano, New Zealand

sharply against a high cliff, dug the blade hard in hopes I didn't smash into the wall. I managed, but only barely, and the river turned left and right, spraying my head, lifting the kayak, a thick wash of water spinning through a maze of rocks.

Once I succeeded in running the Tongariro on that first test ride the ranger promoted me to a three-day ride down the Wanganui. It was even wilder for an old Virginia farmboy, wilder and wetter, and while there were moments when I wasn't absolutely sure of my own survival, there were many moments of bliss, as well, such as the first time I ever heard the raggedy cry of the flightless nocturnal bird that gave New Zealanders their nickname, the kiwi.

At the end of my stay with the generous innkeeper who provided free room and lodging I wheeled my bike to Taupo and set out over a pile of forbidding hills to the southeast. At one point the hills rose to such an angle that I was forced to crank down to my lowest gear.

"She's a big hill, she is, mate," a weatherbeaten man in a civilian car yelled as he slowed some. "I'll pull you with me rope."

Up we went, moving at not more than fifteen miles an hour, my bicycle roped to the rear bumper, an effortless spin through the heat haze. I coasted the other side, free-wheeling much of the way, before hiding my transportation in some bushes and walking a few miles along a remote beach where I found a rest hut with all the fixings for a healing cup of hot tea.

At Cape Kidnappers I saw gannet birds, big, with golden heads, white bodies and black-tipped wings, awkward birds walking on the rocks, light and graceful as a feather when they are airborne. Before planing into flight, however, the gannet shuffles its feet, lifts its neck

Freedom of the river—Wanganui River, New Zealand

and wings high. After that preliminary windup the bird runs swiftly for the edge of a cliff and launches into flight for a bit of fishing.

My parents told me about the birds and bees when I was no bigger than a hoot owl, but they never told me about the gannet. When the gannet comes back from fishing he and his mate stand on tiptoes, breast to breast, their wings stretched open, their necks fully extended. The bills clash for a few long moments and then the heads come together for what looks like romance multiplied to the level of ecstasy.

In the north and south of New Zealand I added other wildlife to the Lloyd Sumner Global Zoo I was filing away in my memory. I photographed some seals sunning themselves on a rocky shore, saw my first penguins in the wild near Moeraki. After a flock of the white-bellied penguins swam in from the sea, one of them treated me to some sort of a ritual tribal dance, bowing, opening its beak, raising its head, the whole body vibrating like a blender, spooky, guttural sounds rising throughout the performance.

But probably the most intriguing bird I saw in New Zealand—or anywhere else on my world tour, for that matter—appeared on a

Gannet colony, Cape Kidnappers, New Zealand

The author and a yellow-eyed penguin at Shag Point, New Zealand study each other at close range.

lonely mountain road beyond Devil's Elbow. All of a sudden a car braked to a stop just ahead of me.

A dream of a girl jumped out, tall, barefoot, her golden hair loose. She was smiling, smiling, smiling, but her eyes reflected an infinite sadness. She clutched a bright red apple in each hand, wordlessly wrapped my fingers around the apples as she peered me straight in the eye.

When her fingers touched mine I felt a current, a jolt of electricity, a strange sense of intimacy. I didn't know quite what to say. "Thanks," I finally murmured. "Thanks."

She squeezed my hand briefly.

"Take care, take care," she said in a soft pleading voice.

Then she ran to the car, opened the door and disappeared forever. I couldn't fathom the mystical experience. I still can't. All I know is that it haunted me for several days—and I have never tasted sweeter apples.

"Open your mouth." The dental surgeon in Gisborne peered into my mouth in search of the ailing tooth that brought me to his office. "That one looks bad, very bad. It will have to go."

The dentist was a big man, big and strong, so muscular he probably could extract a tooth with one of his thick, sausage-sized fingers. He ordered me to move my tongue to the right, reached for a needle, shot my gum full of something supposed to be anaesthetic.

"It's probably numb by now." He opened a pair of large pliers, got a grip on the suspect tooth. "Come out." He was having a hard time

The little hole that was patched before the big hole finally burst the tire for good, East Cape road, New Zealand

of it despite his impressive size. "Come out, bloody tooth." Something loosened. "Ah, there it is, a long tooth, the longest I've ever pulled, I think."

But it ought to have been even longer if he'd lived up to the diploma framed on the office wall. That dentist in Gisborne didn't get all of that tooth. By actual count seven remnants of his hard-fisted attack worked their way out of my mouth over the next month. My mouth was especially sore that first sleepless night—and I felt the pain of it for several days.

When another tire blew a few days later I found that the worn old tube simply wouldn't take another patch. My options came down to the obvious. I stuck out my thumb in hopes of hitching a ride into the nearest town for a visit to the bike shop. A truck driver asked me to throw the bicycle up back and accompany him to Rotorua.

As he drummed along a two-strip roadway a sheep-shearer acquaintance and his wife I had met several days earlier passed by in their car, spotted me through the window, flagged us down. They insisted I join them, leaving my bike, my pack, my cameras, even my passport and travelers' checks in the back of a truck driven by a man whose name we didn't even know. People frequently do things like that in the innocent new land of New Zealand.

But the country was crowded with something more than a rigid sense of morality. I saw rainbow trout more than two feet long swim clear water, I watched tribal maoris do ritual dances, I ate foods I had never sampled, shot rolls of film of vents, geysers and deep waterfalls.

Before long I even joined forces with a fellow bicycle addict, Bruce, a whipcord man of around sixty with a white beard and a long hawk of a nose. He greeted me with a grunt and a disdainful scowl, his ferret eyes registering acute distrust from the very start. But soon he started talking, endlessly talking, talking many different things, a long rambling monologue lighted with bite and profanity.

"You a pommy bastard?" He employed a fairly pejorative term for the English as we wheeled north on the Firth of Thames.

"No. I come from America."

"Damn Yank."

He paused briefly, probably reflecting on the fact that I didn't fit the image of rich Americans. But his silence didn't last for long.

"I have everything a man could ever want," he said. "I listen to music on me wireless and recharge me batteries as I bicycle along. Me tent, which is worth fifteen hundred dollars, it keeps me dry and—"

"Hold on." I couldn't help but swing at such a fat pitch. "How do you figure the tent is worth fifteen hundred dollars?"

"That's how much it saved me in rent. Anyway, I have me stove for cooking, and I'm a bloody good cook. I even make me own gas, using fish waste, but I'm not telling you how I do it. I've been many years learning these things, and people act nasty when I can't tell them in two words how they can find a paradise, too."

The old boy had lived on his bike for ten years without ever leaving the north island of New Zealand. He knew a great deal about wild foods, but he also planted crops as he traveled, returning to each patch at exactly harvest time the following year. He caught fish for himself and his cat Snow. Every now and then Snow returned the favor by bringing Bruce a fresh-killed bird.

"Snow is me second best friend in the world," he said. "The first is Him up there. They are the only ones worth a grain of salt. I'm one of the few people who can tell the rest of the world to go to hell and mean it. Buggar them all. I don't need anybody."

As he explained it at excessive length, it became clear why Bruce didn't need anybody besides his white cat. He spends a total of $1.30 a week, which he considers fairly profligate in view of his carefree past. Before he took to cycling he once walked more than 1,000 miles at an outlay of merely five cents. He found the coin on the road, invested it in an ice cream cone. Until he was arrested for dealing in secondhand goods without a license, he used to support his rambles by collecting bottles.

"I put a curse on the arresting officer, a strong curse," he told me. "Two weeks later, he was badly beaten and cut by a drunk who swung a broken bottle. So Him up there is just."

After I was out of earshot of the nimble old self-provider I caught a launch with another acquaintance for Poor Knights Island, which stood twelve miles offshore. We couldn't legally land because the island is the home of the tuatara, living fossils of the reptile family, an endangered species, which isn't surprising, because their ancestry reaches back into the tall grasses of prehistory, 200 million years ago, even before the age of the dinosaurs.

With our launch carefully anchored a hundred yards from shore in clear water, my mate Marshall patiently explained how simple scuba diving was. I wasn't altogether convinced, especially remembering skin diving in Hawaii. Swimming with a heavy awkward pack on my back, flippers strapped to my feet, wasn't natural for a home-grown mountainboy. But at least it seemed worth a try.

As I lowered myself over the side and psyched up for a trip down

Bruce, Snow, and their $1500 tent on the Firth of Thames, New Zealand

into the lower depths Marshall remembered one last thing. He handed me a belt, a weighted twelve-pound belt.

"It will help you sink," he said.

"I know. That's just what bothers me."

Once I finally let go I sunk very nicely. I sunk 10 feet, 20 feet, 30 feet. Even in my wet suit the water was cold. The mouthpiece bit deep into my gums. The mask filled with water. I came to the surface for the necessary adjustments, went skinning back down again.

At thirty feet the pressure set my ears to aching. Remembering Marshall's directions, I held my nose and blew hard. Something popped somewhere. Strange noises spun through my head, discordant music, all of it out of tune, but the earache was gone. Instead of peering up for a reassuring look at the surface, I began to explore the beauties down around me. With a kick of my flippers I saw the underwater world in three marvelous dimensions, saw the magnificent colors and shapes, saw a layer of seaweed, lichen and coral on a spire deeper down.

All around me I saw fish in a riot of colors, bright reds, yellows, golds, greens and browns. Sometimes they came so close I tickled their bellies. If my talkative bicycle chum Bruce ever discovered a way to hand-build his own scuba gear, he'd probably tickle those fish right into his frying pan.

Riding toward Mount Sefton in Mount Cook National Park, New Zealand

Scuba diving was tremendous, same as the mountain climbs, the green land stretching away, the whole of New Zealand. Scuba diving was tremendous but mostly I saw the sights on my bicycle. By the time I spanned the breadth of the two islands my odometer registered 11,717.6 miles.

But after all the fascinating miles, after all the new patches on the tires, after all the vivid experiences filtering into my memory, it was time to leave. I'd lost a tooth, most of a tooth, anyway, but I had found another country beyond the limits of my Virginia horizons.

In the end I experienced some mixed emotions about New Zealand. The tour through its infinite variety of stunning scenery, encounters with people generally so friendly, sights of penguins and experiences like the scuba diving rise pleasantly in my memory even today. But as I gradually discovered, New Zealand is part of the real world too, the same as other countries, with social, political and environmental problems of its own. If it existed at all, the true promised land still lay ahead.

Besides, Australia was singing a siren song of its own just a short flight away.

Chapter 6

Australia East

Australia is an enormous country only in terms of its land mass. It's big, almost as big as the continental United States, and yet the total population runs to only 13 million people. Eighty-five percent of those people inhabit a few large cities, while the rest of Australia amounts to great sheets of open country, wild and filled with excitement, which struck me as a very nice ratio for a stranger in search of sights to see.

But first I needed the cities, for several reasons, not the least of them the fact that they could produce the income I needed to accumulate for my tour of Australia, Asia and Africa. On the basis of my experience in New Zealand, which had made me self-supporting again, I employed exactly the same technique in Sydney and other large cities. I'd contact newspapers about stories, television stations about appearances, universities and computer groups about lectures on computer art.

Meanwhile, I also began learning the language.

"We saw you pedaling through this arvo and wondered if you were fair dunkum," a whipcord little man with a nose the size of a tangerine said.

Translation: arvo—afternoon; fair dunkum—serious, for real.

"You going on your pushbike back o'Bourke?" another wondered.

Translation: through the remote outback.

"Well, bloke, you got Buckley's."

Translation: no chance at all.

On learning that a ship bound for Melbourne was due to leave Sydney a few days later I hurriedly revised my informal itinerary. I would commence the trip in Melbourne, ride to Darwin via Sydney and Brisbane, south to north, in other words, instead of east to west.

Quite apart from a number of acquaintances I had originally met in New Zealand putting their homes and dining rooms at my disposal, Melbourne was a grand success. In three weeks I gave two lectures, produced a computer-animated movie at a university, did four hours with the Australian Broadcasting Company filming a program for national television, saw a game of footy, or Australian Rules Football, rougher than our brand, and explored the Victorian Alps.

Life was enjoyable and easy in Melbourne. I might easily have stayed another month just accepting invitations already received, but three weeks of the easy life is about the limit of my endurance. I promised my friends "See you next time around" and rode east on Highway 1.

Things happened fast. A few cars stopped to offer tea, sweets, and good wishes, but faces in other cars were sour and scowling. Suddenly, a wolf whistle was blown my way. I thought that some ruffian was trying to be smart but turned to see three pretty, giggling girls. A little later on a small country road—zoom, zoom, zoom, zoom, zoom—five motorcyclists whizzed past. Then one by one they all stopped, turned around, came back, and surrounded me. They had seen me on television and wanted to ask a few questions. Yes, I was fair dunkum, and yes, I was enjoying my trip.

A few miles farther along a motorcycle and two carloads of drinking youths were parked in the road, forming a roadblock. One snarled at me, "Where the hell you going?"

"Around the world."

"Whatcha riding a pushbike for?"

"Got no better sense, I guess."

"You're American, aintcha?"

"Yeah, but I was pretty little when it happened and couldn't do anything about it."

"Well, here, have some beer." Someone tossed a bottle to me. A little humor had kept me out of trouble.

A few days later I faced still another threatening confrontation. While I rested, something huge crashed through the peaceful eucalyptus forest. Startled, I turned as an emu pranced into view. Normally I would not have worried, but I learned that among emus the tallest is the boss, and pecking order is a constant concern. Since this emu was taller than I was, he charged as I tried to take a picture. Emu

The emu that wanted to peck my eyes out, near Lakes Entrance, Victoria, Australia

beaks can be vicious. I had no place to run, but I knew a trick. By holding an arm over my head, I became "taller" than he was, and he backed away fearfully. When I lowered my arm to focus the camera, he charged arrogantly at me again. Another hand in the air conjured up another frightened, and somewhat confused, emu. This little game continued until I rode swiftly away, still holding my hand aloft—emus can run over thirty miles per hour.

In another encounter with Australia's unique wildlife, I spotted the cuddly koala bear, the very picture of innocence, asleep in the fork of a low tree. Wanting a better picture, I shook the branch a little. The round ball of dense gray fur wrinkled its leathery nose, opened one eye, looked accusingly at me, and urinated in my direction.

Mount Kosciusko, Australia's highest peak, was now within cycling distance, and the snow was reportedly good. In Perisher Valley, the access point for Mount Kosciusko, I met Peter Hart and John Hooper, who loaned me ski mountaineering equipment, then decided to attempt the ascent with me. The Snowy Mountains glistened and we hit a fast, exhilarating gait in a world of pure white.

After a cold night in Seaman's Hut, a memorial to Lawrence Seaman, an American who froze to death nearby, we carried our skis across hard crusted snow on the hazardous traverses.

Leaving the skis below the last big slope, we climbed to the top by kicking steps into the crust. The summit offered superb views of the Great Dividing Range, sensuous white mounds rolling to every horizon massaged by fogs rising from the valleys.

Going down was exciting. Control on that icy crust would be impossible. We all held back, laughing at our predicament, wondering how to negotiate the impossible slope, waiting for someone else to take the lead. Finally, John led off. After a hesitant step or two, his feet went out from under him and his body bobsledded for lower country. Down he went, down, down, sliding faster and faster, disappearing over a shoulder, scooting again into view long seconds later. Peter and I watched John's spread-eagled body finally stop, 750 vertical feet below us. We could see he had slid harmlessly into a broad saddle. I took the sleigh ride next, and Peter soon followed. It was an unparalleled thrill; we even considered climbing the slope and falling again.

The ride to Sydney was peaceful, quiet, and pleasant.

Sydney was good to me. I visited in several wonderful homes, gave four lectures, was commissioned by IBM to do two new paintings. On the computer time they provided, I also did a drawing of Maria, which sold almost before I had a chance to sign it. My lecture to the Australian Computer Society was so successful that they invited me to return six months later with my multimedia show for a price virtually guaranteeing the financial resources to get through Asia and Africa.

At one of the lectures I met Doug Richardson, short, full-bearded, mild-mannered, impulsive, a singer, and a computer artist, who offered to introduce me to the sport of canyoning. We acquired the necessary ropes and slings, drove to the Blue Mountains, and bushwhacked toward a gentle U-shaped valley. Tall, overlapping trees hid the deep, narrow canyon at the bottom. After rappelling down a pair of 100-foot vertical cliffs, we reached the water and began our tramp downstream. It got exciting when I slid over the first waterfall and

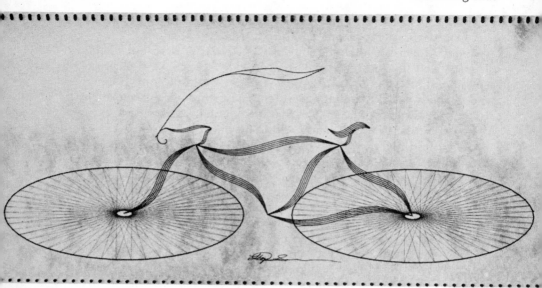

Computer art portrait of Maria

dropped into a deep pool. Unable to touch bottom, I tried to swim but became entangled in the rope. After performing a Houdini escape, I still had to swim fully clothed and carrying a pack in ice-cold water until I reached a gravel bar thirty yards away.

The canyon narrowed, almost becoming a tunnel between the cliffs far above. The next waterfall required sliding headfirst with the gushing water through a small hole in the rocks, then a tricky move to land on a sloping, moss-covered ledge at the head of a long pool. After I swam it my teeth chattered, my body shook violently, and I could not get warm again.

When we came to the biggest waterfall of all, followed by a still longer swim, we decided that if we continued, the unpleasant climax of our trip would be death by freezing. The slippery waterfalls blocked a retreat.

From the looks of things our only hope was to climb the sheer cliffs hung straight over the river. But the rock looked loose, splintery, precarious. We were trapped, in other words, trapped without a prayer of climbing back out unless we crossed the rock on hands and knees along a shallow ledge to a side canyon. Even that looked beyond us.

Perhaps we could reach an upper canyon and muck our way up a spindling snowgum. Perhaps. Even if we managed that, however, we'd have to catwalk an upper branch to still another ledge and hope there was a route from there.

Still, we went moving cautiously up, ascending each cliff with a crabby lack of speed, feeling our way, hoping, hoping the holds wouldn't let go. Somehow they didn't, although I don't know why to this day. We made it up to the top and out of a trap neither one of us was certain we could escape.

After our canyoning adventure Doug Richardson decided he'd like to bike with me for the next six weeks. He bought a bike, trained by riding it home from the shop, and hitched a ride north until he caught up with me.

Several days later we were riding along a back road—flat, treelined, with one paved lane down the center. Doug, behind me, sang at the top of his lungs, and I really felt good as I pedaled peacefully along. I thought of the pros and cons of having a companion. There were a few drawbacks! I did not get invited into as many homes, was not as free to alter plans or pace. But it added interest in other ways; I had another viewpoint to clarify some strange happenings, such as my encounter that day with the sugar cane trucks.

The first truck was heavily loaded and coming toward me. I waved as usual, but the driver's eyes seemed riveted on the road ahead. He did not wave back, and I felt snubbed. Seconds later, an empty truck passed me from behind skimming by just inches away. I thought that rather discourteous.

But Doug saw the drama differently. Here, as he described it is what really happened.

> The truck was moving too fast. Making the deafening racket of an empty truck on a corduroy road, it passed me with half its wheels churning mud on the shoulder. As it swung back to the pavement, I saw that it completely filled this one-lane Queensland road. About 300 yards ahead, Lloyd was still pedaling his bicycle along the edge of the pavement. He did not see the truck behind him pull half off the pavement on his side of the road—he would be caught dead center. It was senseless murder, and all I could do was watch. Then I understood. A loaded cane truck was coming the other way. If they passed soon enough, the empty truck might have time to avoid hitting Lloyd. The two trucks passed with no room to spare, but as they passed, the empty truck went into a skid. It slid sideways down the edge of the road, the back wheels clawing desperately to gain traction on the soft clay shoulder. It would be an accident, but Lloyd would be just as dead. I watched anxiously for what seemed like an eternity, until the truck was finally back on the pavement, swung out and avoided Lloyd by the narrowest of margins and left him pedaling peacefully on.

That incident makes me wonder what other near disasters unfolded without my knowledge.

A day or two down the road we met the most bizarre character I ran across on my whole journey. He stopped his car in the middle of the road, jumped out and tossed a half-empty stubby of beer to Doug. The short, shabbily dressed, heavily smoking man eyed us critically from a safe distance, jerking his head from side to side as he sized us up. Finally, he thrust his hand at me. "My name is Tom. I'm a wild man." He then blew his nose with one finger to prove it. He ran back to his car and extracted a shy, frightened, five-week-old puppy. "This is Kevin. He's a wonder dog."

After persuading Tom to park his car off the road, we joined him for a few beers and listened to his stories. Tom claimed he had been a prisoner of war of the Japanese, had made and lost three fortunes, had $187,000 which came from "the well," was a "religious alcoholic," and had a friend named Peter, a Russian Jew. "Peter has fought for five armies (he always switches sides if his side is losing), has killed 3,000 men, is hung heavy, and can talk at 40 feet under water with a mango in his mouth. He even puts a bucket of cow manure in his living room to keep the flies out of the kitchen."

During the monolog, which ranged over many subjects and was well punctuated with X-rated expletives, Tom would leap up, punch the air, make threatening gestures, but reassured, "Don't worry, I'd never touch your body." Then he jumped in his car and left.

Half an hour later we were again stopped by Tom the wild man and his wonder dog Kevin. He brought us each a quart of lemonade and suggested we should marry the barmaid in the next pub, then conceded that she might not want to marry us.

Tom invited us to his house in Gladstone for a cup of tea. It was eighteen miles out of our way but sounded like an adventure, or at least a misadventure. We arrived at his house two hours later and were surprised to find Tom mowing the lawn, looking like a typical suburbanite. "Come in, youse two. Meet my wife."

His wife was sick in bed and seemed fairly normal. Tom found a coffee can, relieved himself in it in front of all of us, and emptied it out the window. He then left to make the pot of tea, but not in the coffee can, I made sure.

Suddenly, Peter, Tom's swashbuckling Russian friend, stormed into the room without knocking, sending wonder dog Kevin diving beneath the sofa. He spit through his coal-black beard and cursed nonstop for forty-five seconds. His 270 pounds swayed on his six-foot-six frame; he was drunk. He was the meanest-looking man I had ever seen. Tom's earlier descriptions of him were emphatically understated. Doug and I tried our best humor routines, but Peter remained stone-faced and was loudly critical of our soft life. He challenged Doug, who is a very good player, to a game of chess for a dollar. Peter did not concentrate on the game, preferring to make vulgar passes at Tom's wife. But even so, he won the game and the dollar. Perhaps Doug was being tactful. When Tom finally appeared with the tea, the cup was cracked and dirty, the tea was overly strong and sweet.

Tom offered us a bed for the night but we declined. He left with us, a Bible in his hand. Tom the wild man was on his way to church. We cycled about the dark city for an hour before finding a "Bed and Breakfast" house for the night.

Doug and I traveled to Cairns for a few days' exploration of the Great Barrier Reef. When I rolled Doug out of bed at dawn, he protested, claiming we were wasting good sleeping time just to visit the wharf on the chance of catching a boat to the reef. But I had a feeling that morning—something good was brewing, I had no doubts at all.

Doug was right. No boats were going to the reef that morning, but a forty-four-foot ocean-going ketch carried a sign, "Crewmen Wanted." I had never sailed but had often dreamed of it. The thin, rather pale owner sat in the captain's chair and described the job. "I need two crewmen to sail with me across the Indian and Atlantic oceans to Florida. I pay $200 a month plus all expenses."

This was too good to be true! Usually one has to share expenses for the privilege of going along. I applied for the job on the spot. If I got the job I would sail to Florida and use the money earned to fly back to Australia and continue my bicycle trip. Doug agreed to take Maria back to Sydney.

There were twelve other applicants, all with more experience than I had, but Henry Kawecki admired my venturesome spirit. "You and I are made of the same kind of stuff," he said. "How soon can you move in?"

I couldn't remember being more excited. The vision of this magnificent vessel sailing gracefully across the great expanses of ocean—the vision of tropical islands, remote places, storms—and I would be part of that. I was a crewman on the *Wayward Wind*. I bought a bottle of champagne and bubbled enthusiastically over the possibilities. Doug pointed out the captain's frail health, and I wondered, too, what might happen if severe illness struck any of us on the open sea.

Henry Kawecki, sixty-one, had worked hard—too hard—all his life to rise from near poverty to owner of an 80 million dollar business producing rare metals. Now he was retired and living his dream of sailing around the world. His wife Clara, who did not share his love of sailing, traveled with Henry only because she was completely devoted to him. She had a kind, grandmotherly appearance. The other crew member was Michael, six-feet four, 210 pounds, with long blond hair and beard, that made him look like Neptune himself.

I could not have dreamed of a greater trip. The weather was warm and clear. The only sounds were made by wind and waves. The beauty of the *Wayward Wind* under full sail was breathtaking. We only sailed a few hours each day, using the rest of the day to explore uninhabited

Maria pauses to inspect the Sydney Opera House and the Sydney Harbor Bridge, Australia

islands and to dive over the coral reefs. We found glass fishing floats, the nest of a sea eagle, the wreck of a World War II airplane and an endless variety of colorful seashells. Each day we caught a fifteen- to 30-pound tuna or bonito for the evening meal. Once I shot a nice blue-striped grunt with Henry's spear gun, the only one in the world with a tantalum tip.

After a week of leisurely cruising we anchored for a few days at Lizard Island, an island some two and a half miles across boasting a 1,179-foot peak. Unlike the other islands we had visited it had an airstrip and an inhabitant, Peter Falkes, who had two-way radio contact with Australia's Flying Doctor Service.

Henry and I took the dinghy to shore early one morning to leave some letters for Peter to mail when a plane visited. "Why not move over to the next bay," I suggested. "It's better protected."

"No, I want to be closer to Peter, closer to the radio, closer to the airstrip," Henry said. I vaguely wondered why he cared and dropped the subject.

At noon on our second day there I helped Clara make a pot of stew. Henry suddenly said, "Clara, I feel a little dizzy," and fainted.

He revived once, took a sip of water, asked if he had passed out once or twice, then collapsed. Michael tried mouth-to-mouth resuscitation, I massaged his heart, and Clara prayed. It looked bad—Henry was not responding. Clara sent Michael to get Peter while I continued the mouth-to-mouth resuscitation, working methodically, trying not to panic. My right arm holding Henry went to sleep and my mouth ached acutely from the constant pressure. It seemed that Michael was taking forever.

Unknown to us, the outboard motor had run out of gas, and Michael was being blown out to sea. The dinghy was very unstable under Michael's heavy, jerky movements and he nearly fell overboard while trying to refuel it. Finally he was able to refill the tank and restart the motor. Peter called the flying doctor, got explicit instructions, and sped back to the *Wayward Wind*.

I knew already our captain was dead. I had felt his spirit depart. We could find no pulse and his pupils did not respond to light. There being nothing else we could do on board, we carried Henry to the motorboat, and Peter and Michael took him to shore. The doctor was already on his way.

I stayed on board to console Clara as best I could. We prayed together, read from the Bible, and talked of their good times, of their children and grandchildren. I reminded her of how much greater it is to die quickly, painlessly, and doing what one loves to do rather than a prolonged death in a hospital.

The doctor arrived within an hour. Clara flew with the body back to Cairns, leaving Michael and me the "next of kin to the *Wayward Wind*."

Temporarily, at least, we were marooned, but Lizard Island is a good place to be marooned. It has long powdery white sand beaches, sheer granite cliffs, a variety of vegetation, no poisonous animals or insects, not even mosquitoes, and is ringed by deep-blue, coral-laced waters. As the days passed we relaxed and alternated watching the ship and exploring the island. At night Michael smoked his pipe and played softly on his guitar while I sat in the captain's seat and gazed at the stars, wondering, but not really caring to know, what destiny they held for me.

Clara returned briefly to get some personal things and to say that a new captain would be engaged eventually to pilot us back to Cairns. We were simply to boat-sit until we heard further.

Next morning I swam the quarter-mile to shore. When I arrived, Peter asked if I were racing the twelve-foot hammerhead shark that cruised those waters almost daily. Noting my lack of concern, he confirmed what I had always believed—that the danger from sharks is so slight it is not worth considering. He had seen sharks while diving. One zipped by his head not two feet away to take a fish off his spear. Another swam up to him, sniffed at him, then swam away.

I enjoyed my days alone on the island. I walked the long beaches, climbed the granite cliffs, ran through the soft, swaying grasses, explored the rain forest and chased three-foot goanna lizards. I ate the abundant oysters, passion fruit, coconuts, papayas, and yams. Often I stripped naked to swim in the warm clear water or run along the deserted sands. I was free. And I got sunburned in places I had never been burned before.

One day I climbed above the sheer cliffs and pushed into dense jungle. I crawled through the tangled vines and roots, getting well scratched by the briars and well bitten by green ants. Once on the cliff edge, I moved quickly to avoid a new nest of ants and lost my footing. I would have suffered a bad fall, possibly a few hundred feet into the sea, if I had not been saved by, of all things, spider webs. The sticky, half-millimeter-thick strands were matted together so tightly that I could not see through them. It took a good bit of my strength to break the strands and release myself.

Exploring the coral reefs was even more exciting. The underwater world of the Great Barrier Reef is more varied and brilliantly colored than I had seen in Hawaii or New Zealand. That, along with my much improved swimming and diving ability, kept me as excited as a kid at an amusement park as I dived again and again to visit the gently swaying tentacles of delicate feather starfish, the deep blue-green pulsating mantle of giant clams four feet across. I swam with the fish, drifted with the sea anemones, and came to feel completely at home, but every couple of minutes my bursting lungs reminded me that I was only a visitor in this world.

On our tenth day at Lizard Island, Captain Roy Adams arrived to pilot us back to Cairns. Our Robinson Crusoe idyll ended—too soon.

Days later, in the tumult of Sydney, I was riding through rush-hour traffic when a car turned sharply into a parking space. Rubber burned, metal tore, my pulse lurched into another beat. The collision catapulted me into the air. The bike and I made a complete flip, with the bike rising in one direction and myself in another, before I landed on my back and somersaulted to my feet. For reasons I can't understand to this day, the bike and I came out of the wreck without a scratch, while damage to the car was estimated at $200.

Somehow that near thing seemed an appropriate end to several potential perils I had managed to avoid along the fascinating way through the east of Australia.

Chapter 7

Australia Outback

It was still sticky-hot after dark when I arrived in Kalgoorlie to begin my tour of Australia's famous outback. I wondered about the wisdom of cycling across deserts in late summer as I wiped away the sweat and rode off to seek lodging.

"Where can I find a bed?" I asked the publican behind the bar.

He eyed me curiously, smiled broadly, and said, "Down on Hay Street, fifteen dollars for five minutes."

I considered the price a bit exorbitant even after I realized what he was referring to. "No, no, no. I'm looking for a place to *sleep*."

"You came to Kalgoorlie to sleep?! Well, it takes all kinds. Try the Nullarbor Guest House. Three dollars for all night, but you have to sleep alone."

Next morning the air was more nearly tolerable. I bought some emergency food and a half-gallon of orange juice before rolling into the desert country. Twenty-five miles of uninhabited, rolling, sparsely forested hills quickly melted away as I pedaled into Coolgardie. The first person I met in this "living ghost town" asked, "What do you think of Coolbloodygardie?"

"Well, it's the best town I've seen since Kalbloodygoorlie."

"Yes, she's a beaut," he beamed, not catching my double-talk.

Years ago Coolgardie had a population of 20,000, including Herbert Hoover when he was a young mining engineer, but is now down to 500. Behind its old facade is a modern town with a swimming pool, where I lounged as the temperature soared to 104°F. On a side trip at sunset I met a pair of cycling lizards. When disturbed they run on their back legs, with motion like that of a person riding a bicycle. I felt an especially close communion with these little fellows.

After a night at the youth hostel I was up at 5 A.M. and on the road before dawn. It was almost cool and I felt good. And then Maria picked up the first of several unwelcome hitchhikers. A mean plant called the double-G grows in this area, and its seedpods have sharp thorns on all sides. I fixed two punctures in the dark and quickly rode on to pass as many miles as possible before sunrise. The temperature began to soar, and so did my spirit. This was Australia: no settlements for 100 miles, empty roads, empty sky, a few snakes and lizards, red dirt and gum trees. There were no billboards, no houses, no fences, not even dead animals on the road. I hadn't felt so good in months.

The road was an endless succession of rises and dips. Climb one rise, see the next. Climb that one, and see rise after rise after rise. Once two kangaroos stood in the middle of the road and stared without understanding as I slipped between them.

By noon the sun was menacing. I should stop and wait for cooler air, having ridden eighty miles already. But a small sign enticed: "Joe's Roadhouse—Ice Cold Drinks—20 Miles." The sun gave me a throbbing headache and I slowed my pace to half its morning rate. The ecstasy of the morning was gone.

By riding only five miles at a stretch, with long rests in the shade of gum trees, I managed to roll into Joe's Roadhouse oasis, where Joe's thermometer read 108°F. Joe, a wiry old man in overalls and a floppy hat, met me at the door with a Coke so cold that ice was floating on it. He was the only human resident of the town of Yellowdine. I gladly accepted his invitation to spend the night with his family: dogs, cats, goats, sheep, showy parrots called galahs, ducks, chickens, and turkeys, all sharing his half-acre lot. I carried six buckets of ice well water to pour in an old tub for a bath before Joe's delicious dinner.

Next morning, after a cup of Joe's fine tea, I was off for another fast, thrilling ride in the cool air. Flocks of galahs and Port Lincoln parrots flew along with me for miles at a time, squawking their excitement at the strange sight I made. The air was pure and sweet, and I sped tirelessly across the Australian countryside. Small, sparsely stocked stores appeared every twenty to thirty miles, and I stopped at each one and had several of whatever they had. At Cerrabin I was enjoying a steak-and-kidney pie when a local rushed into the store. "That your pushbike out front?"

"Yeah."

Joe, Joe's Roadhouse, and part of Joe's family, Yellowdine, Western Australia

"You'd better come quickly. There's a bloke all dressed up in pink and gray trying to steal it."

I rushed out to find a galah giving Maria a thorough inspection. After I gave him a ride around the station, he let me depart.

Like the previous afternoon, this one became stifling hot. After ninety-five miles I reached Merredin and an unwise combination of several kinds of liquids caused my head to fog, my stomach to churn. As the Australians say, I was "crook." After a few minutes of lying down, I "came right" but decided to splurge on a motel room and have a good rest.

In next morning's cool air I felt great and despite the promise of a headwind and another hot day, I turned south toward Wave Rock. The road was narrow, treelined, and a flyway for clouds of parrots. The traffic was heavier than I expected—about three cars an hour. At Narembeen I cut back east on a road with only one car an hour. Later I turned onto a gravel road where I did not see a single vehicle for five hours. By afternoon I was in real outback country. But there

A galah hitchhiker, Cerrabin, Western Australia

were occasional farm ponds, and I swam in every one of them to cool off.

I rode the 103 miles to Hyden by sunset. The local kids made me an instant hero and organized a fifteen-bicycle escort to travel with me the last two miles to Wave Rock.

I pitched my tent in the dark, and as I cooked my evening meal, a six-foot, upright figure suddenly appeared, moving slowly, smoothly, quietly straight toward me. It cannot be a kangaroo, I thought; kangaroos must move both legs at the same time, and this causes a noisy jerky hop. So what was this creature, now close enough to have me well frightened. I relaxed when my intruder entered my firelight and I saw that it *was* a kangaroo. I had forgotten, or never knew, that they can balance on their tail while moving their legs slowly and quietly forward. He was looking for a handout and a warm body to sleep beside. I shared a few bites of stew before we lay down side by side for the night.

Wave Rock, sculpted by wind-driven sand, is some 300 feet long and 60 feet high, curving smoothly into an overhang, a great petrified

Kangaroos, too, have to scratch when it itches.

Maria becomes a surfboard as the author "shoots the curl" of Wave Rock, Hyden, Western Australia.

tidal wave poised to break across the desert. It was overwhelming, rising starkly out of the desert, well worth the blistering detour.

I left at noon and rode for the fifth straight day through temperatures exceeding 100°F. After 64 miles of desert riding I carried the bike to the top of Gorge Rock, a 200-foot-high rounded block of granite. I patched a tube in the dark, ate a cold supper, and relaxed to enjoy the celestial extravaganza. The perfectly still, unpolluted desert air revealed more stars than I had ever seen before. The landscape around me was illuminated by the dazzling dome of sky, more white than black. There was such a profusion of minor stars that even major constellations were hard to recognize.

Blessed by a following wind and temperatures only in the 90s, the ride was fast and easy on to Perth, a lovely city of many parks, sparkling white buildings and grassy-banked waterways.

There I turned Maria south along the Indian Ocean. The air was cooler and the countryside greener, but heavy traffic, rough roads, and intensive developments were depressing.

By midafternoon I had drunk all my water and was thirsty again. I stopped at a country pub where I was quickly adopted by three locals. Little Pom, Little Bastard, and Big Aussie invited me to lay over for the weekend, and after renaming me Crazy Yank, introduced me to the pub mascot, Umpy the Camel. Umpy descended from the thousands of camels brought from India and Afghanistan to aid in desert exploration, prospecting, and in construction of the Nullarbor Railroad. At one time 12,000 or more camels worked in Australia. Now, most of their descendants, in herds of tens of thousands, run wild in the northern deserts—the only wild camels in the world. Umpy, I soon discovered, had a wild streak in him, too. While talking to Little Pom, I casually scratched Umpy's hump. He snapped around, took a nip out of my arm! That was the first of several bites I was to suffer in the next few months.

I rode away late Sunday morning more fatigued than when I stopped at the pub. The traffic was heavy and hostile, the crosswind strong and tricky. The back tire, with only 800 miles on it, blew out. Two speeding cars forced me off the road. My head ached with a dull throb, brought on by drinking too much. I vowed to limit future pub stops to an hour and tuned my ears to the songs of black cockatoos.

I rode ninety miles to Quindalup, and there shed my shoes for a walk down a quiet beach at sunset. A small beagle came along and I welcomed the company. When I turned to go back the dog ran ahead, stole my right shoe and disappeared in the darkness. In searching for

my missing shoe I found a left-footed flipflop and wore it on my right
foot for the fifty miles on to Margaret River, the nearest place that
sold shoes. It doesn't pay to get up some days.

Two days later, a motorcyclist passed, then stopped well ahead. He
held something high in the air. Oh boy, food, I thought, but when I
pulled alongside I saw he held my missing shoe. Richard Speak, a
short, black-haired Englishman, had been at Quindalup after me. The
hostel warden had found my shoe and given it to him to deliver.

Richard and I exchanged a few notes on two-wheel travel. He was
dressed in heavy jeans and down parka and complained of the cold.
I wore shorts and T-shirt and thought it hot. He said he had seen only
one kangaroo in nine months of touring Australia. I boasted about
twenty I had seen just that morning. No question about it, I decided—
a bicycle is the way to travel.

I pedaled over the Porongorups and Stirling ranges, took a side trip
to climb Bluff Knoll, the second highest peak in western Australia.
Coasting down the steep access road at 60 mph, confident that no cars
were coming, I laid Maria acutely into a blind curve. Suddenly a
wallaby was squarely in my path. A collision would probably be fatal
for both of us. He sat up, pricked his ears, but failed to move. I swung
left. He hopped left. I swung back right. He hopped back right. Too
late for further maneuvering, I faced directly at him. There was no
thud, just a fluttering as his wildly swinging tail harped across the front
wheel spokes. Somehow the bike held the road.

Days later—on Easter Sunday, in fact—none of the small towns
along the way were open, and I began to worry that my provisions
might run out. Surely at Grass Patch, I thought, there will be an open
store. Not so. Grass Patch had one store and one hotel and both were
closed. Very tired from struggling against the thirty-knot wind, I was
debating what to do when a car pulled in. An effervescent lady hopped
out to check her mail and then asked about my trip.

"We're having our traditional Easter Sunday cricket match and
barbecue. Would you care to join us? I'm sure the boys would like to
meet you. And if you need a place to sleep, you're welcome to use our
caravan." Once again my luck had held out.

Rested and well fed, I rolled ninety miles to Norseman, the jumping-
off point for the Nullarbor. From there to Penong, 716 miles away,
there would be no post office, police station, doctor—just an occasional
filling station, restaurant, and hotel. The first such one-building
"town," Balladonia, was 120 miles away. I would not be able to find

even water before then. I forwarded a few extra clothes and camera lens to make room for the one and a half gallons of water and food for three days I decided I would need.

When I began planning my bicycle trip around the world, I looked at a map of Australia and was awed by the road across the Nullarbor. How would I handle the heat, the dust, the aloneness? Could I carry enough provisions? Would bike, body, and mind stand up to the continuous pounding?

I promised myself that I would not attempt the Nullarbor unless I had a following wind. But good judgment was shoved aside by curiosity and enthusiasm, and in the morning I was thirty miles down the road before the wind asserted its direction. The air, however, was bitter cold; I improvised mittens with my extra pair of socks. The countryside was rolling and covered with low bronzed bark gum trees. The road was hilly. There were no animals or bird life.

I pedaled steadily, but ran out of light fifteen miles short of Balladonia. As I was about to decide to stop and camp, a fast-approaching pair of lights screeched to a halt. Out jumped Chris Lait, bartender at Balladonia. He said he had heard all day about the bicyclist getting closer, and his curiosity would not let him wait. He jumped around excitedly and kept repeating, "I don't believe it. You are fair dunkum. I don't believe it." He insisted that I must ride on to Balladonia that night and promised to come back looking for me if I did not arrive in two hours.

Chris sped away, leaving me alone in the silent darkness. Having no light, I guided on the centerline, just barely visible. I pedaled on, slowly, quietly, enjoying the peaceful desert night. Half a mile ahead were the lights of the building, and soon a shout, "Here he comes," pierced the stillness. I was an instant hero. Chris handed me the largest beer he had. At least twenty cameras captured my surprised, but well-pleased, face. Children asked for my autograph. Four fellows from Melbourne insisted on buying my dinner—a sixteen-ounce T-bone steak—and all the beer I could drink. This business of roughing it across the Nullarbor was off to a good start.

The next morning was one of the most moody and beautiful that I have ever known. It was still quite dark when I started riding. Two stars and a sliver of moon hung in the sky ahead. Ground mist veiled the roadside. It was an eerie, soul-uplifting ride.

My reception at Caiguna was somewhat less enthusiastic than at Balladonia. No one offered me a smile, a glass of water or the time of day. I bought a few soft drinks and rolled on, no longer a hero. I had not intended to reach Madura that night, but in midafternoon a sudden burst of energy stimulated my legs, and I was only ten miles away when I stopped to admire the sunset. The serenity was flawed by a hissing sound, a tire was leaking air. Not wanting to take time to fix it, I chose to pump and sprint. Pump the tire. Pump the pedals. Pump the tire. Pump the pedals.

I pushed on, lured by visions of a shower and a bed, and finally hobbled into Madura.

"How much for a room?" I asked.

"Sorry, mate, we're full up."

"But I've ridden my pushbike 124 miles today, and I sure need a place to sleep."

A trucker, hearing my tale of woe, offered to share his room. The shower was a disappointment; the salt water left me stickier than when I entered it. The soft bed, however, was pure heaven.

Another early start, another moody, misty morning, another exuberant ride through another 114 miles of the desert brought me to Eucla. Eucla, notorious for once recording 123.9°F., the highest ever in Australia, was the end of the paved road. I tightened all nuts and bolts before dining with an elderly man and his daughter. They described the next 240 miles of unsealed road as "a random hodgepodge of mud, dust, water, rocks, limestone blocks, mired trucks, and potholes you can lose a car in."

Next morning I began. I attacked the road right down the middle, bouncing through rocks, mud, and dirt. Road conditions varied greatly. Some parts were so good that I could ride at top speed. On other parts my average speed was about three miles per hour. As the road became rougher, motorists became friendlier because they were going slower. They regularly stopped to offer food, drink, rides and advice on the road ahead.

Then came the first of the waterholes. I splashed on through, feeling sorry for the cars mired in the mud on the side. Some of these impromptu lakes were 200 yards long and a foot or more deep. The main problem was in not knowing when the front wheel would drop into a rim-bending or car-swallowing chuckhole. Still, riding in water is much preferable to riding in the bulldust which usually covers the road.

If I had seen the vastness of the Nullarbor Plain from a plane I probably would have shuddered at the thought of crossing it on a bicycle. But, taken a few miles at a time, not seeing more than ten miles ahead, I didn't feel overwhelmed or intimidated by its size. I never tired of the country. I loved its vastness, its virginity, loveliness and its subtle beauty.

Alone on the Nullarbor Plain, South Australia

After a night alone in the middle of the Nullarbor I had one of my greatest days. The desert, flatter than the sea, stretched to infinity in every direction. The air was pure and cool, the road rough but passable. And I met the friendliest drivers on any road that I have ever ridden. That day I reached a new high in enjoyment and communion with land, bike, and people.

Most of the cars that stopped were equipped with 'roo bars to protect the radiator in collisions with kangaroos, which are too common at night. One old man told of a young Englishman who drove this road without a 'roo bar. He collided with a big red kangaroo, leaving his car severely damaged and the kangaroo apparently quite dead. As a joke the driver dressed the kangaroo in his hat and coat, propped it against the bashed car, and went for his camera. The kangaroo re-

Maria becomes a bucking bronco in the bulldust of Queensland, Australia.

vived, and leaped swiftly away with the coat, and his wallet with about $500 in it.

Because of the dozens of people wanting to talk, take my picture, and offer me food and drink, Maria recorded only 71 miles that day, making 698 miles in the last 7 days. The highlight of this day of great friendliness was rolling into Ivy Tanks. Max and Nat Fuss were full of questions and I was full of answers. But I was also hungry. My face fell when I spotted a sign, "Meals No Longer Served."

"Oh, I sure was looking forward to a warm meal."

"We're closing down our restaurant service, but anyone who has done what you have deserves a feed, so we'll make an exception."

Next day I dared take my eyes from the wracking road and saw a band of wild aborigines waving boomerangs over their heads. Oh boy, I was in no condition to do battle with the natives. But as I cycled closer I saw that they wanted to sell a boomerang to me, not sail a boomerang at me. I noticed a particularly well-carved one.

"How much?"

"Four dollars."

I counteroffered two cans of beer. The withered old lady snatched the beer, thrust the boomerang into my hand, and ran swiftly away before I changed my mind. Then the whole tribe descended, offering great bargains in carved kangaroos, wombats and eagles for a single can of beer, but I had no more and had to ride swiftly away before they ripped apart my packs to be sure.

Despite various troubles, my spirits stayed high until I reached a paved surface a day later. Then depression, the first in a long time, set in. Cars whizzed by without stopping. The bike rattled and squealed, the headwind became stronger, and the countryside was uninteresting farmland. But I pedaled the few more miles to Penong, thus completing my Nullarbor crossing. I had proved my ability to cycle long distances and carry sufficient food and water for at least 250 miles at a time. I hadn't only survived the Nullarbor, I had very much enjoyed it. I never met a motorist willing to make that statement.

I caught a train back to Sydney, where I exhibited my computer art. Later, on the train to Alice Springs I met Margaret Honey, a girl whose philosophies closely resembled my own. She had a car, a gentle manner, and was set to travel indefinitely.

In Alice Springs I went to collect my bicycle.

"You're not Mr. Sumner, by any chance, are you?"

"Most everybody calls me Lloyd, but yes, that's me."

"Oh, dear. We just had a telex from Perth. Your bicycle failed to change trains in Port Pirie. It should be on its way back, but we haven't heard anything since."

Margaret's pretty face creased in a smile. "Now you have no choice," she said. "Now you have to come with me to Ayer's Rock."

Soon after leaving Alice Springs it was clear that we were not seeing the area in its usual condition. The Red Center was not red; the Dead Heart was not dead. Heavier-than-normal rains had left the countryside green, grass waist-high, and huge fields of wild flowers swaying in the breeze. We drove straight to Ayer's Rock, the largest monolith in the world. Rising 1,100 feet from the flat surrounding desert, this hunk of red granite is five miles around, a spectacle to amaze even the most choosy of scenery watchers. We drove to the far

Boomerang-making aborigines of the Nullarbor Plain, Australia

side, parked the car, and started climbing a well-marked trail. The climb was straightforward and easy, with hand chains for the steepest parts. From the top we saw miles and miles of flat plains and the Olgas, a cluster of some thirty rounded reddish domes, several of them higher than Ayer's Rock.

All next day we wandered among the Olgas. We walked the Valley of Mice Women past the Dome of Dying Kangaroo Man and Pillar of Lizard Woman. Surprisingly, we found dense jungles, waterfalls, and swamps among the immense red rocks. Several times we heard a sound like a sudden strong wind as a flock of several hundred parrots buzzed us in perfect formation. Then another flock would zip through from another direction, their yellow-green coloring brilliant against the shadows on the rocks. Once we saw six separate flocks flying at great speed, turning sharply in perfect unison. We were so infatuated with the wonders of the Olgas that darkness caught us in the Valley of the Winds, and only luck led us back to the car, preventing a bivouac without even coats for warmth.

In a lush oasis known as the Garden of Eden, nestled in the barren walls of King's Canyon, the two of us seemed the only people in the world, beyond the limits of civilization, past the edges of humanity, nothing less than Adam and Eve. We climbed a low ridge to watch the sun set on our private kingdom. A solitary ghost gum, its white bark glowing against rich red ochre hues of the canyon, stood nearby. Margaret took my hand as a kaleidoscope of colors cascaded down the canyon walls, ending in a misty purple glow, the stars filling every corner of the moonless sky. She didn't bother setting up her own tent that night.

On our return to Alice Springs Margaret and I talked of ways of continuing the happiness we had found. I suggested she trade her car for a bicycle and a plane ticket, but she didn't want to go abroad until she had seen Australia. She suggested we go live on Lizard Island for a few months or years. The idea was tempting, but I felt I had to complete my two-wheel trip around the world. Being equally headstrong, neither of us gave in.

Our decision to part saddened me; Margaret was a lovely woman, a fine companion, and she had done wonders for my ego. I had been preoccupied so long with reaching the next goal on my wandering that I rarely found time for a normal relationship.

I said a reluctant "See you next time around" and pedaled north toward Darwin, 963 miles away. Despite the long layoff from cycling, my muscles never complained as they pushed Maria eighty-four miles to Aileron by early afternoon. There, in the Aileron pub I met one of the oddest characters of my trip. Yvonne, an attractive, swashbuckling female, was easily dominating all the men present. When the subject came to Love, Yvonne said, "Bloody hell, I've been married four times and lived in sin with another man or two and never have been in love. Hey, you in the fancy shirt [me], what do you think of that?"

"Me, I've been in love four times and never have been married."

"What the hell is love anyway?"

"Well, I've heard it described as a condition of the mind when the mind is out of condition."

"Yeah, I'll buy that, and I'll buy a beer. Come on over here where I can talk to you. You going up or down?"

"Up."

"How about giving me a lift to Ti Tree?"

"I'd like to help you, but you've obviously not seen how I'm traveling."

"I can fit in anywhere."

"Even on a pushbike?"

"Aw, you're kidding."

"Go see for yourself."

"Bloody hell, I thought I was the only one who did that."

"You mean you ride a bicycle?"

"Rode one 483 miles once, averaging 45 miles a day. Not bad, eh?"

"Pretty good going. Where was this?"

"West from Sydney. Four of us got drunk one night and decided to do it. We bought bicycles for about ten dollars each and took off. We made quite a sight. I carried my little white poodle in a basket. There was also my Dane, who spoke with a Yankee accent, and a Maori girl, who was very fat and very black, and then the Hungarian. When we hit one town a drunk raised his head and said, 'Holy hell, the circus done come to town.'"

"Did you have any problems?"

"Only with the Hungarian. He insisted on speaking English with everyone he met."

"What's wrong with that?"

"The only word of English he knew was that in-and-out word. Why do you ride a pushbike?"

"It's a good way to meet the local people."

"Oh, mate, there's some characters in this country. Meet old George here. Show him your neck, George."

George leaned over to reveal a deep scar around the back of his neck. "He stole some chickens from the Chinese, and they tried to cut his head off. And then there is Olaf here. He's from Norway, a sailor for fifty years. Tell him why you settled in Aileron, Olaf."

"I wanted to get as bloody far from the bloody sea as I could bloody get."

"You like characters, eh? Well, I'm going to show you to Flo. She's the original Australian. The first time I met Flo was in this pub. She stormed in mad as a crocodile, grabbed a truckie twice her size, and knocked him leg up. She said, 'You hit me bloody cow, ye bastard, and you'll pay for it one way or t'other!'"

In the middle of this discussion, Max, a new Australian from Yugoslavia, walked in. Yvonne pounced quickly, and he agreed to drive us to Ti Tree to meet Flo. Yvonne purchased a large supply of beer and we were off with a warning, "Don't mind Flo's language. She's no daughter of a preacher. She might call you a few names or slap you leg up, but she's a good person really, one of the best mates I got." At Ti Tree Max and I listened, amazed and amused, as Yvonne and Flo exchanged all the latest gossip. Their language would have made the devil blush, but they treated Max and me kindly. Flo, the squinty-eyed, shabbily dressed, double-brandy-drinking boss of Ti Tree society, handed me a sandwich, "'Yar, mate, wrap yer laughing gear around that."

Yvonne showed me around Flo's farm. "Now this cow is Matilda. She is the only Jersey cow in the territory. And this is Little Bull. I caught him myself. He fell out of a truck and I grabbed him and wrestled him to the ground. We were waltzing all over the place."

"You mean Little Bull was waltzing Yvonne and now he's waltzing Matilda?" "That's a good one, Virginia [Yvonne's nickname for me]. Have another beer."

Pushed by a nice following wind, I made good time over the next few days. The mornings were bitter cold despite the tropics.

Late one day I stopped beside a car with trouble. The petite, dark-haired solo driver was almost in tears when I couldn't fix her burst oil line. Finally along came a familiar vehicle—Max the Yugoslav, who agreed to tow her to the next station.

I cycled north through country painted golden yellow by many species of wattle in full bloom. Among the wattle and the taller gum trees were anthills up to fifteen feet tall. Some looked like sand castles, some like cypress knees, morel mushrooms, stalagmites, abstract sculpture, and tombstones.

More than 115 miles up the road that day I came upon a familiar

Yvonne and Flo, the two most beautiful ladies in all of Ti Tree, Northern Territory, Australia

sight, a lone female and a disabled car. As I cycled toward her, the spry, gray-haired lady said, "You fix my car and I'll drive you to Katherine."

"Well, I'll be glad to fix your tire, but I don't want a ride."

She was insistent. "Oh please, I'm all alone and I'm frightened now that it's almost dark."

"I think you'd like my oldest daughter," she told me. "She is beautiful, intelligent, and positively charming, but, poor thing, has trouble getting married. Her first groom-to-be was murdered two weeks before the wedding. The next was killed in an automobile accident on his way to the church. The third died in a mining accident just shortly after setting the wedding date."

"Sounds like Somebody Up There doesn't want her to marry. Where is she now?"

"In the hospital. She and her fourth husband-to-be were both seriously injured in a car wreck a fortnight ago."

At dusk on the shortest day of the year I laid my sleeping bag in virgin bush amidst the thumping of kangaroos and a varied bird symphony. It was my last night in outback Australia. Darwin was just 100 miles away. From there on I didn't know quite what to expect.

In Darwin I got shots, visas, travelers checks, a money belt, a larger medical kit, new tires and hopefully a new mental attitude for the "other half" of the world.

On one of my last days I met Jim, a Russian-Australian, and his Balinese wife Nuriti who planned to sail to Bali in a few days. Jim said he couldn't take me because the *Alvis*, a forty-four-foot sloop, was old, his lifeboat only held two, and space was limited. I kept hoping while I finished other business, and three days later Jim agreed to take me at least as far as Dili, Timor.

Australia was great to the very end. I had cycled over 7,000 miles, stayed twice as long as originally intended, made many new friends, and enjoyed a few unparalleled experiences: the soul-uplifting aloneness of the Nullarbor; being marooned on Lizard Island; and the star-studded nights of the deserts. But, Australians, as well as New Zealanders, had values, life-styles, and attitudes similar to those in America. I was overdue for a major change. Now I looked forward—with certain misgivings, admittedly—to Southeast Asia and Eastern culture.

Chapter 8

Timor, Sumbawa, and Bali

As a landlubber type generally rooted to the sweet land in and around Charlottesville, Virginia I am not what anyone might describe as a saltwater sailor accustomed to leaning into the wind. This qualification seemed especially significant when the vessel I rode was a dated forty-four-foot sloop carrying three people and a rickety lifeboat built for only two.

Yet, surprisingly, I thrived on the nautical life as we sailed for Timor and Bali. I took my turn standing watch, learned more about reading a compass, reflected on where I had been and where I was going under the great bowl of sky salted with stars. On our fourth day out I managed to hoist Captain Jim, a great sack of muscle, up in a bosun's chair to repair a damaged stay supporting the mast.

Even some heavy weather failed to daunt my exhilaration during our leisurely passage toward Bali. After we turned the corner of Timor the sea rose like a cliff, waves beating over the bow, drenching the three of us, the *Alvis* heeled nearly horizontal. In the ominous wash of all that water I found myself whooping with joy.

Our arrival in the magnificent bay off the north coast couldn't have been more appropriate. Four natives in an outrigger canoe paddled straight for us, tied up to the stern of our sloop. While a language barrier I was to encounter too many times the next two years flattened any conversation with three of the smiling greeters, the fourth spoke just enough English to express their sentiments, which were touching, as we learned on offering to buy fish or coconuts from them.

"No got fish," the official spokesman replied. "But we get you coconuts. No want money. Want friends."

If they sold us coconuts their relationship with us would be commercial. But if they gave us coconuts the relationship would be social. In their view friendship was to be valued more highly than money. It was a lovely distinction, I thought.

Now that our relationship had been so carefully defined, Captain

Natives of a remote coastal village on Timor and their dugout canoe used to board the Alvis

Jim saw no reason not to give each of them a cigarette and a stick of gum. The cigarettes were familiar enough, but the strange gum presented tactical problems. One of our instant friends saved his as a souvenir, another folded and filed in his pocket the strips of wrapper he carefully tore off, still another put the gift in his mouth, chewed and swallowed, wrapper and all.

Our entry was every bit as memorable as that experience with the four Welcome Dugout natives. In the peaceful harbor of Dili government buildings gleamed white against a painted blue sky, a magnificent high-steepled church rose off to our right. Eastern world, here I come, I thought as we sculled the dinghy ashore.

A crowd of children watched while I bolted my bicycle back together. They were happy kids, happy and friendly, their eyes a-goggle despite the fact that we couldn't communicate. I smiled and spun off, laid on a three-course Chinese meal and had an experimental go at my first Eastern toilet. The toilet consists of a hole cut in the floor and tread marks indicating the proper position for the feet.

In Timor the single most important event is the weekly cockfight, which I decided to watch by way of sopping up some local culture, despite a chronic aversion to blood sports. Four-inch blades are wound tightly against the cock's left foot, owner/trainers give mouth-to-beak resuscitation and then spit palm wine down the bird's throat between rounds, the competition comes to an end any time blood is drawn. I admit to going a bit qualmy when a young white cock, blood spurting from a fatal wound, stretched on its toes and then toppled backwards like the bad guy in some movie shootout.

As happens at sporting events both east and west, the spectators were as intriguing as the contestants. Tattered men who didn't look like they had the equivalent of a dime to their names flashed thick wads of paper money placing bets on their favorite cocks. During the fights normally docile and peaceful men worked themselves into a blithering frenzy. For every winner there was a loser in the gallery as well as in the pit, of course, which meant that the crowd noises were compounded of anguish and jubilation.

Even the most manic spectator can be forgiven some emotional excesses with two thoroughbred cocks rising to slash at one another, but generally natives were far more diffident during the week. If their chronic generosity and good cheer were an accurate gauge of what I was to find in that remote corner of the world, an especially happy leg of my long tour was to follow. Along with their blithe spirit, the Timorese also happened to be law-abiding people with a flinty sense of property rights.

Yet I felt the wind of one deviation from those customary good manners. I felt the wind of it—and it cost me something quite special.

My hat probably didn't look like much. It was old, worn, conical, made of black felt, a perfectly basic hat except for a coating of ornamental patches of organizations I had belonged to over the years. It didn't look like much, but I loved that hat as much as anything I owned.

We had been through a lot together too, the hat and I, not only back home in America but also on this eye-opening adventure cycling around the world. It shaded the sun, helped ward off the cold, covered me on mountain climbs, desert crossings, boat rides and air flights. On many a chill night in Alaska and the continental United States I zipped myself in my sleeping bag with the hat pulled down over my ears.

Aside from its utilitarian and sentimental value the hat wasn't really worth anything, which meant that it didn't intrude on my personal philosophy regarding worldly goods. I have a strong feeling that a person ought never own anything he can't afford to lose. Even in my modest circumstances I could afford to lose that special hat, although, for a number of reasons I can't logically explain, it amounted to my single most valuable possession.

Whatever our cultural and educational differences, a surprising number of people in Timor shared my fondness for that old black hat. My camping gear, my cameras, even my bicycle interested them far less than the hat, as they indicated again while I shopped for supplies in the colorful marketplace in Dili. If those pleasant and otherwise decent people couldn't manage to skin it off my head, they tried to buy it for what were obviously impressive price levels in an economy where bananas retailed for a penny and a comfortable hotel room for only $1.

"One hundred escuedos, I give a hundred escuedos," or some $4 U.S., an earnest Timorese shaped like a linebacker offered.

When I told him the hat wasn't for sale he inflated his original bid, up to 100 escuedos and two blankets, to 100 escuedos and four blankets, to 100 escuedos, four blankets and a full stem of bananas, before a tantalizing final offer. He also was willing to include his wife. Although I hadn't met the lady, this struck me as rather excessive.

Assigned to buy a ten-day supply of fruit, I was able to load everything onto the bike—and also fend off natives grabbing for my hat—except for a papaya the size of a football. A crowd of spectators sympathetically reacted as I tried to shove it into a bag, under the brake cable, on the handlebars, all without success. They wildly applauded when, at the risk of looking a pregnant mammal, I stuffed it up the front of my shirt.

At a Chinese shop I subsequently stopped by for canned meats and vegetables the crowd was more boisterous, less friendly. Briefly, very briefly, I laid my hat on the counter to reach for a tin of stewed chicken. When I turned around it was gone, nowhere in sight. The crowd closed in, walling me off, preventing me from chasing the thief, and that was the last I ever saw of my favorite hat, although I expect it's been seen under new management in Timor since then.

Sailing north from Timor into Indonesian waters, we came upon more and more native ships, hundreds of them spread across the sea, small craft rigged with hand-sewn sails and carrying no lights of any sort. They were a problem by day, a real danger by night.

One of them might have been even more than that. It came straight for us, a large, heavily patched sail furled in the wind. It came straight for us for more than an hour. Once it got so close that we could see the crew, tough-looking men, grim and scowling. Pirates intent on boarding the *Alvis?* We never knew for sure. But on the off-chance they were, in a corner of the world where piracy still flourishes, we ran hard until we left them far astern.

The small native sailing ships crowding the water were almost as self-sufficient as transatlantic steamships. They carried milk goats and a few chickens, an occasional tomato plant, whole families in some cases, their own prostitutes in others. Together, they supplied most of the 13,360 islands of Indonesia.

On our third day out of Timor we hoisted the big Genoa jib to catch more of a light wind and settled back to enjoy the tranquil beat of our cruise. Only the tranquil beat didn't last for long. A storm blew out of the sunset, the wind rising from ten to forty knots in five turbulent minutes, and caught us without a warning. Captain Jim struggled to drop the Genoa, raise the storm jib and reef the main sail while I did my best to hold the sloop into the wind.

My sense of excitement, rising like the wind, tailed off some when I saw Jim's face in a wash of light. It was bleached white. And he knew about tropical storms. Years before Jim had fought a hurricane at sea for 96 hours before putting in at Christmas Island. If Jim was visibly apprehensive about the heavy weather around us, I ought to be scared stiff.

Certainly the sea did little to reassure me. In the dark it rose like a roller-coaster, churning, rumbling, lifting the stern out of the water every few washes. I braced myself in the cockpit, the salt spray burning my face, still feeling an edge of excitement, trying to ignore the fact that the small sloop already had twenty-six years on her and my promise not to request space in the two-man lifeboat if she went down. When my watch was over I tied myself in my bunk and fell asleep.

Two days later we ran into another storm, thick and menacing, every bit as bad as the first. The main sail reefed to a sixth its normal size, the spotlight illuminating the night in search of any stray native craft without lights, we crashed ahead at five knots, the waves foaming high over us in the open sea. It got to be a very long night.

By the time we put into the bay at Bima on the island of Sumbawa the sea was calm and gentle. Captain Jim and his native wife Nuriti rowed ashore, leaving me to ward off any visitors despite a jangling language gap, which took some doing the first time two visitors paddled an outrigger alongside.

"Jangan!" I put a bite in the word, went right through the dictionary with what I hoped was the same air of command. "Polisi! Immigrazi! Doctor!"

Something—I never knew quite what—clicked in their mind. They stared at me, pushed off and paddled away. Several others came by without stopping when I intoned the same magic words.

With the salt still burning in my throat, my first commercial transaction in the booming little coastal town of Bima was a soft drink. It was a local brand, elaborately labeled, sickly sweet, with a rancid aftertaste, a disaster, especially after my thirst was so wound up. To slake that foul taste I promptly reached for an absolute, a familiar bottle marked 7-Up, and guzzled. But it tasted exactly the same as the other. So I learned my first lesson in Bima on the isle of Sumbawa. In Bima they simply fill any available bottles with the local concoction, the formula for which I'd rather not even guess at.

But when I started walking the colorful streets of Bima with Jim's wife Nuriti things improved considerably. A number of her old friends lived in and around the town, and they invited us to stop by for tea, coffee or sweetened goat's milk. They chatted away in Indonesian while I sat there smiling, especially at the toothsome daughters, such an ornamental feature of practically every household. As outlanders, presumably fairly high up the social scale, we were invariably seated in the inner ring with members of the immediate family, while relatives sat in a second circle beyond us and respected members of the community in a catch-all outer ring.

At meals I tried to conform to the local level of table manners, which took some doing. As an old resident before she packed off with Jim, Nuriti, a spectacular-looking girl with large brown eyes, long dark hair and a mouthful of perfect sparkling teeth, knew exactly how to behave. At the end of every meal she emitted a resounding no-nonsense belch. Whatever its social impact elsewhere, the belch is considered a required tribute following a successful dinner in Sumbawa.

Before we left, Jim and I accompanied Nuriti when she called on a Hindu priest for some special prayers at a temple rising high over Bima. She spent several hours carefully dressing for the occasion, but she didn't have a special maroon sash, which meant she would have to pray to Vishnu the Preserver instead of to Brahma the Supreme Creator. In view of her great needs, the three of us were distressed that she had to settle for less.

What Nuriti specifically wanted to pray for was an end to the chronic seasickness that beset her even in the calmest, flattest seas. My own time aboard ships wasn't extensive, of course, but I had never known anyone to suffer such miseries. Nuriti spent most of her time hanging over a rail, emptying herself, and she couldn't eat or sleep when the boat was in motion.

A thick-set Hindu priest listened attentively while Nuriti described the problem that cursed her. He and his four-year-old daughter knelt with her in the sunshine atop the hill alongside the temple, blessed the flowers and food she carried on a basket balanced on her head. For almost ten minutes they asked Vishnu's blessings.

On our way back down the hill I asked the priest why they prayed in the open instead of in the temple. His answer struck me as altogether sensible. Hindus don't want a wall or ceiling to intrude on their prayers to the particular deity they are addressing.

The first night we put to sea again Nuriti sacrificed two sacred flowers and fell asleep in the companionway. She slept like a top right through the night. Next morning she awakened refreshed and free of her terrible old torment.

"Small white boy, he come to me during the night, say 'go inside, Balinese never sleep in doorway,'" she explained, the wonder of it showing in her dark eyes. "Small white boy go inside my body, make me well, make me sleep."

Preposterous? It sounded preposterous as we sailed the sea that morning. Yet for the rest of our voyage Nuriti invariably ate full meals, got a full ration of sleep and wasn't sick even once, even when we hit some heavy weather. On the basis of that close-up demonstration I saw for myself, Hinduism seemed an intriguing religion.

At first two eyeballs appeared in the blue-green water on our port side. They looked enormous, huge and unblinking, riding through the sea, big as cantaloupe. Scaled to size, however, they weren't actually big at all.

A prodigious head slid to the surface, blunt, colored a dark gray. Gradually the whole body appeared not more than twenty feet away. Once Captain Jim, Nuriti and I saw the whole of it we realized that the sperm whale was a good ten feet longer than our sloop, which was perfectly all right as long as it kept its distance.

For a few numbing moments the whale cruised right along with us, blowing water, fanning his tail. We felt fragile, fragile and vulnerable, a small boat in a big sea inhabited by this and other hazards. But soon the whale went into a long leisurely dive and disappeared.

Otherwise the four-day trip on to Bali was uneventful. In the soft glow of dusk Nuriti taught me some rudimentary language skills. Among other things, I learned how to count in another tongue: *satu, dua, tiga, empat, lima* . . .

She also expressed her reactions to Australia. "Australia me no like." Nuriti assessed countries by her own scale of values. "No festival, no good rice, no market. Bali good market, good rice, many festival."

Despite the gaudy testimonials she and others offered up—"It's as close to paradise as you can ever find," a man back in Australia had told me—a skeptical suspicion rose in my mind. Bali couldn't possibly measure up to all the extravagant tributes. But as we sailed into Benoa Bay, dropped the anchor and rowed ashore I hoped desperately that it would.

The first thing that filled my eyes were barebreasted women moving along the streets, which seemed an inconsistency only because miniskirts so prevalent elsewhere in the world are not legal in Bali. It was mostly native women who bared their breasts, but young Europeans go topless on Kuta Beach, too. After the first pleasant shock of it wore off, I found the de rigueur style was beautifully natural rather than erotic.

The roadways were crowded with pedestrians, cyclists, horses, motorcycles, three-wheeler taxis and large Chevrolets. A girl carrying a full bushel of oranges on her head cycled past me, braked to a stop, rushed to her place in the market without so much as touching the basket with her hands.

Camping there on the wharf for the night might be dangerous because it was a rough area, at least for Bali. At an illegal house of prostitution catering largely to the seafaring traffic I wasn't able to convince several plump, heavily painted ladies that I wanted a room for the night—and nothing more. With the sun beginning to melt down in the harbor I jumped on my bike and set off for Kuta seven miles away.

At the first losman—small hotel—in Kuta the manager neglected to ask for my passport, which was just as well, because I had yet to officially check in with the immigration office. When I finally did I was given a thirty-day visa and asked to purchase an outbound ticket to my next stop, Singapore.

Early my second morning in Bali I came upon a crowd of men chanting and singing while they carried a tall colorful bamboo tower up the middle of the road. Every few moments they stopped, lifted their singing several decibels and spun the tower round and round. Further down the road I saw another tower, brighter still, and another, and another.

A young boy standing by the roadside noticed that I was perplexed. "Cremation, celebration, festival," he said. "Over three hundred bodies. Come along."

According to my youthful guide, the Balinese believe the soul cannot be released until the body is burned. Poor people might not be able to afford the expensive ceremony for years, but priests must be cremated at once. So any time a priest dies, people dig up the bodies of their loved ones to be cremated with the priest, with his spirit escorting the other spirits into heaven, a sort of celestial hitchhike.

The bodies scheduled to be burned were racked high in the colorful towers. The ritual of turning the towers was designed to confuse the spirit to a point where it couldn't find its way back home and haunt the surviving family. In Bali people take ghosts seriously. They even go so far as to build special baffle gates outside their homes because ghosts are said to have trouble turning corners in the dark.

In Bali cremations are a festive occasion and interesting to watch, up to a point. I reached that point not long after they set fire to a great wooden bull holding the remains of the priest, along with the tall towers carrying all the other cadavers. Just when the fires got to burning nicely, just when juices began to run from the roasting bodies, a young boy working the crowd tried to sell me a local drink.

On my way to the mountains I stopped to visit Nuriti and her family in the village of Pelitan. Her mother, naked from the waist north, greeted me with an exuberant handshake while children, chickens and pigs scratched in the yard outside. Her father, a sensitive man who supports his large family on some $250 a year, which he earns as a

Cremation tower on main highway between Denpensar and Kuta, Bali, Indonesia

professional woodcarver, is not rich or famous even by artistic standards, although he seemed a contented man.

Over a cup of tea he explained why I had seen so many examples of artistry in the villages I'd been cycling through. According to him, the Balinese believe that God created a very special place in Bali, gave it to them as protectors. By way of offering up abiding thanks, the people spare no effort in creating art, music and dance. Art and religion mingle, with practically everyone an artist of one kind or another. Even dirt farmers who manually plow the land all day keep the faith by carving ornamental woods by night.

On the steps of a temple at Ubud I had a brief encounter with a wild monkey, although it wasn't quite brief enough. For a long moment he reflectively peered at me. Then he toddled over, sat on my kneecap and explored my pockets, presumably for peanuts, or wild potatoes, or maybe a banana. When he found nothing of interest, he gave me a painful bite on the arm—the same arm a camel had already marked.

Cycling higher and higher in the mountains, I found fewer animals, even more magnificent country and a stronger reaction from the people. They were unfailingly friendly, unfailingly gentle and kind. Old men and women, their teeth stained red from chewing betel nut, smiled and waved as I passed on some spectacular twist of road.

Because I frequently stopped to admire the perfection of the elaborately terraced rice fields, or to focus on caves, shrines and temples, I had to ride the last few miles to Penaloken after dark. It had been uphill most of the day, thirty-one miles uphill. Like a doctor who X-rays a new patient's wallet as well as his shoulder before quoting a price, the lady who ran the losman where I stopped looked outside to check my transportation. Spotting a bike, she charged me $.65. Travelers who arrive by motorcycle or bus pay double that, she told me, people with cars pay triple.

Even that private 65-cent room wasn't a great bargain for me, not because of the room so much as the background noises that kept me awake. Live geckos rustled on the thatched ceilings scratching for flies and mosquitoes, dogs commenced barking promptly at eleven o'clock at night. I was told the dogs were trying to scare away evil spirits, in case any spirits managed to make it past those special baffle gates.

The Balinese culture was so different, the scenery so spectacular and the language so lilting that I had a difficult time keeping a grip on reality. Any time the shock of it gave me the flutters I found myself a mountain to climb, a lonely beach to walk, a wild track to wheel along.

At Kuta I sampled a mixed grill of indigenous dishes, some of them

The king monkey at the Monkey Jungle, Ubud, Bali, Indonesia

too strong for my modest country taste. Until I learned the trick of washing it down with fresh fruit juices laced with crushed ice, a dish known as sate, which translates as barbecued meat on bamboo skewers dipped in hot spices, was especially trying. I stretched in the sun and swam the warm waters curving in a large crescent out beyond my room.

At night I attended dances at a nearby temple built on a dramatic cliff rising straight out of the sea. The dancing was more dramatic still. Bewitching young girls clad in gold brocade swayed gracefully to the liquid rhythms of xylophones, gongs, bamboo sticks and drums. The feature was the celebrated Ketjak dance, a haunting experience, with a blazing torch the only light and more than 150 men chanting counterpoint while the dancers performed.

One special day an old shipwreck of a man with glittery eyes sat down beside me on a street in Negara. He asked me the usual question.

"Where are you from?"

"America."

"Oh. Watergate. Your Mister Nixon. Did you know he resigned today?"

I hadn't, but I was in no way disappointed to learn the big news. In my view Nixon was always too weak, too selfish, too shallow, too out of touch to preside over such a great nation.

I rode the last twenty-one miles through wild country to Gilamanuk on the western tip of the island. Then I pumped up the plank and onto the ferry to Java for another trip into the unknown.

Bali was lovely, a dream of a land. But even paradise can slow a man down permanently if he lingers too long.

Chapter 9

Java

In Java I knew nothing of the road ahead, but I expected to find food-stalls all along the way as there had been in Bali. Already painfully hungry, I pedaled slowly up a long, hot hill. At the top, a forest with sweet, cool breezes replaced the dense, muggy atmosphere of the open lowlands.

After three hours I emerged from the forest to see red and white banners flying, people cleaning and painting an entire town, and parades everywhere as Indonesia prepared for its Independence Day. I became the feature attraction in two of the parades by accidentally joining up.

In Asembagus the parades had not yet started and the delicious smell of *nasi goreng* perfumed the little street. As I sat at a homemade table on the verandah of the Rumah Makan, several quite lovely girls sat down and chattered away with me, even though they knew no English. I learned that the most talkative of the girls was Tjoe Ay Lina and that she was originally from Bali, and I was able to communicate that I was from America. Otherwise I simply said, "Ja, ja" to anything they asked. As usual a crowd gathered in the nearby courtyard and listened intently.

At one point in our "conversation" the listeners giggled and whispered to each other. Then they fell silent, eyes fixed expectantly on me as I casually said another "Ja, ja" and began eating my *nasi goreng*. As I concentrated on the delicious fried rice mixed with pieces of pork, shrimp, egg, cauliflower and other vegetables, a man emerged from the kitchen and in quite good English said, "You want me to translate?"

"Yes, thanks, that would be nice."

"My daughter says you are very handsome."

I hastened to return the compliment. "And she, sir, is the most beautiful girl I have ever seen in Java."

"That's good, now that you say you will marry her, you must buy her a plane ticket to America. She doesn't want to go by bicycle."

What Jim told me really was true—I could have my choice of Indonesian girls. He said their one ambition in life is to marry a "stranger," as any European is called. They know that marriage to an In-

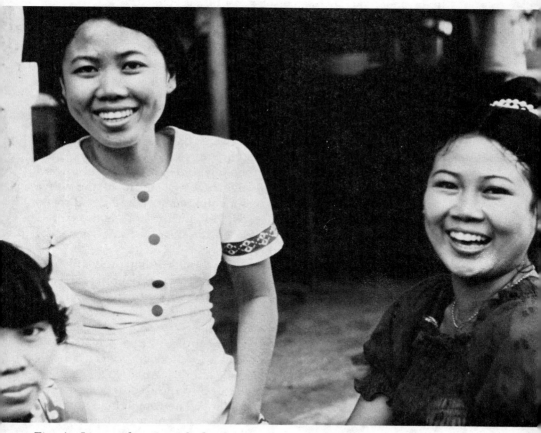

Tjoe Ay Lina, right, after I had unknowingly accepted her proposal for marriage, Asembagus, Java, Indonesia

donesian means living in poverty with stacks of children, stacks of hard work. But, if they marry a stranger they will be whisked off to the West and an expected life of leisure.

I looked at Tjoe Ay and the warmth exuded from her big brown eyes raised my temperature a good two degrees. Her skin color was lighter than mine, her face was round and her long black silky hair was tied neatly in a bun. Her dark blue dress was most becoming and slightly revealing. If marrying a beautiful woman was my goal I would have had to look long and far for her equal. But I knew that she would be unhappy in a land far from her family, where there are no temple festivals, no cremations, no gossippy markets. Yet I would never convince her or her father of that. And the fact remained that I had said "Ja, ja" in a land where a person's word is accepted as law.

Finally I smiled bravely, paid my bill, and explained that it would be two years before I was back in America, unless she came with me now the deal was off. She rushed inside, presumably to pack. I strolled nonchalantly over to my bicycle, then leaped in the saddle and sped quickly away, getting lost in another parade passing on the street.

For the next several days I kept looking over my shoulder to see if anyone was in hot pursuit. And I never again said "Ja, ja" just to be polite.

Next morning I bought the usual twelve bananas for ten cents and ate them for breakfast as I rolled on through more wild country. About noon I rolled into steamy hot Probolinggo, looked longingly toward the cooler mountains. Someone suggested a side trip to the active volcano, Mount Bromo. There was a hotel there where I could spend the night. At the bus station I asked, "Mount Bromo?" and, before I knew it, the bike had been thrown on top of a bus, my bags and I thrown inside on top of the other travelers.

At the end of the line I got the bad news that the hotel was still miles away, ten miles away, in fact. The road was incredibly steep and rough, and it was almost dark. Riding was next to impossible so I pushed where I could, and sometimes practically carried Maria for mile after grueling mile. Many eerie noises—screeches, screams, a rumbling grunt—sounded louder, strange because of the darkness. Suddenly, just in front of me I heard a low warning growl. I froze, thought hard of tigers. Perfect silence. Another growl. "Only a dog," I hoped. I nearly collapsed when a large bird shrieked in the low overhead trees. I heard footsteps approaching. The wandering native was equally scared of me. Then I heard nothing but was surprised by a sudden light in my eyes. Another native scampered behind a tree.

I passed a lonely outpost where one or two men sat around a fire.

When I failed to respond to their shouts, they started beating a drum, perhaps to warn the next village. The stars shone brighter than usual, but it was still very dark. Between me and the mountains flew a brightly lit elliptical object—a UFO. Somehow it seemed right in place.

Then came the last long push, a track so steep I should have been strung with rope. The weight of the bike was almost unbearable. My will to continue was almost nonexistent. Yet I had to go on; there was no place to camp, the land was too steep, the conditions too risky.

At last, lights where the hotel should be. With renewed energy I pushed on to another small village! A young boy grabbed Maria. I asked, "*Hotel Ganung Bromo?*"

"*Satu kilo lagi.*"

Oh no. I couldn't possibly stand another kilometer. Still, if he was wanting to guide me probably he was lying. The distance was probably much shorter. Sure enough, not far away the hotel lights made one of the most beautiful sights I ever hope to see. I didn't even mind the exorbitant price of $1.75. After all, I got a room with a private bath, even the rare luxury of toilet paper.

Despite the long ordeal and late arrival, I was still up next morning to complete the climb of Mount Bromo on foot, hoping to arrive by sunup.

The climb began by descending the outer crater wall, then crossed the Sandsea Desert, and continued up the sharp slopes of the central cone. The roar of the volcano directed my footsteps through the darkness. The first light of dawn turned the great column of steam billowing from the crater a pale blue.

I stood briefly on the crater rim and gazed into the deep, bubbling caldron before climbing higher on the lip to wait for sunrise.

In the dawn a figure approached out of the vapor and sat down beside me. It was Isabelle, a beautiful, intelligent, and venturesome mademoiselle from Paris. Tigers, frightening natives and UFOs I could believe, but a Parisian on the rim of Mount Bromo? This dream was real. Over the rumble of the volcano we talked of our travels. I learned we were going in different directions—she to Bali to purchase artifacts for her sister's shop, and I to America on a bicycle. She invited me to stay with her when I got to Paris.

Isabelle was not the only interesting stranger I met on the slopes of Mount Bromo. After Isabelle and I parted company, I made the acquaintance of a medical student named Budiharso. Pleased at meeting a fellow climber, he invited me to stay at his house when I reached Malang.

At a country fair in Pausaran on my way to Malang I sniffed the wild scents of dried flowers, admired the variety of vegetables on sale in open stalls, sampled some fruits, soft drinks and a bowl of hell's-fire-hot chili. All the time an audience thickened, laughing, watching me, talking a bit, until finally it reached several hundred.

When I made faces at them, they roared with laughter. When I tried singing, the crowd around me enlarged. When I asked if anyone spoke English, nobody answered. Abruptly I experimented with a line of my very limited Indonesian, which provoked a number of questions, none of which I could answer in the native language. All of a sudden the mood changed from revelry to menace. Someone threw a piece of sugar-cane stalk at me, someone else threw a pebble.

With no police around to offer assistance and the adults watching with a wry amusement, I bolted, running as fast as I could, running for my life as the assault continued. I darted between motorcycles, hopped on a horse-drawn cart, leaped over a young cow, sideswiped a betjek loaded with fruit, but the screeches, the cries and the thuds of stones and rocks hurled from the young/old children in pursuit of me continued until I slipped into a foodstall. The shopkeeper blocked the angry crowd at the door, nodded toward the rear. As he kept them distracted I sneaked out through his living quarters, skinned over a fence and returned to the safety of the hotel with my heart still pumping.

A few days later, as the guest of Budiharso in Malang, I saw the sights and enjoyed a supper of martepe, an Arab food of unusual taste and consistency. The next morning my insides felt like I had swallowed a porcupine. Any movement caused intense pain from shoulder blades to lower abdomen. My head felt as if it could explode. I ran a fever of 106 °F., and had a bad case of diarrhea. I do not know if it was food poisoning, bad water, or a curse put on me by someone at Pausaran. None of Budiharso's medicines helped.

Should I telephone for my emergency money to fly home? At the rate my body was disintegrating, I'd be dead before the money arrived.

Then Budiharso's elderly woman servant came in my room, looked at me sympathetically and asked if I would like her to make me well. She was uneducated but a practicing folk doctor, Budiharso said, and a very good one. So I quickly agreed. She rushed off, made an ointment of various herbs and other unknown vile-smelling ingredients. This mixture she scraped into my back with the sharp edge of an old Chinese coin. The scraping was rhythmical, repetitious, accompanied by a low chant.

Within five minutes of her finishing this *kerokan*, I was as good as new except for the scrapes on my back. Porcupine was gone. Headache was gone. Fever was gone. Even diarrhea was gone. I suspect that my recovery was as much due to white magic as to the ointment— or the treatment might have been akin to acupuncture. Needless to say, I am still very grateful to Mbok Nah, whatever the secret of her medicine.

Budiharso, the sensitive gentleman, had suffered along with me, thinking he might have been responsible for my illness. Now he was relieved and kept trying to do that little something extra for "Mister Lloyd." He had already, without my knowing it, thoroughly cleaned and greased Maria and developed my latest roll of film. But that was not enough. Couldn't he also get me a girl? I explained that this girl might be like the ones I heard about in Bali: 5500 rupiah special, 500 for the girl and 5000 for the doctor. His only comment, "I think this doctor price too high."

The only women in the life of a man here are relatives, wife, and prostitutes. The idea of a girlfriend seems immoral to them, but prostitution is quite all right. Also cheaper, more convenient, less frustrating, and less time-consuming than dating, he said. It is also good for the economy. He couldn't understand that I have dozens of friends who happened to be girls.

From Ngawi to Solo I cycled on a special road for nonpolluting traffic, bicycles, betjeks, and animal-pulled carts. I passed long lines of small boys carrying hay, herds of wandering cattle and water buffalo, a crowd cutting sugar cane, old women sometimes bent double from the loads on their backs, and rice laid out on the road to dry.

I was gradually getting to know the genuine Java, a land where people were always staring, watching, touching my hair and skin if they got the chance, and rubbing their hands all over the bicycle.

It wasn't uncommon to see people bathing or relieving themselves in full public view, usually in the river, but no one watches unless the person letting go is a Westerner; then everyone watches, and gives a rousing cheer upon successful completion.

Public eating places have not lost their charm by being overly sanitary. Once, I rode down a long hill parallel to a stream in which people were washing and defecating with no regard to anything downstream. At the bottom of the hill was the only eating establishment within miles. The overly plump lady jovially washed my bowl in the same stream, did not bother to dry it before ladling a serving of rice

Mbok Nah, the "witch" doctor who cured me in five minutes of my most severe attack of illness, and her granddaughter Te, Malang, Java

Bathing time for buffaloes and boys, near Pekalongan, Java, Indonesia

with her big black hand and plopping it down before me. The choice was clear: eat or starve. I ate.

In order to get my visa extended, I cycled to Jogjakarta, a large city with much cultural interest and a center for batik painting and printing. While there, I took side trips to see the great Buddhist temples at Borobadur and Prambanon and into the mountains for a swim in a pure freshwater pool. Otherwise, I didn't stay long in Jogjakarta. It was too full of tourists and beggars for me.

I chose the hardest possible route out of Jogja—a continuous uphill climb for fifty-five miles. At the start, I saw the highest density of bicycles I had ever seen on a road, three or four abreast as thick as possible for ten miles, all of them commuters on their way to work. Up higher, higher still, the road was exclusively mine. A dense cloud cover kept me cool. It later brought heavy rain, the first rain I had seen since Sydney three months before.

I was on my way to Dieng Plateau, said to be the most beautiful part of Java. Among the many mountains are five or six active volcanoes, lakes, lush meadows dotted with ancient Hindu temples. But

I only had time for a quick ride around the plateau before the monsoonlike rain began to pour in sheets.

The people I encountered carried clubs or machete-type knives and had a wildness in their eyes. But their reaction to me was mainly fear. Women, especially, moved well off the road or picked up a bigger club as I passed. I tried to smile assurances but their faces showed only blank, uncomprehending stares.

I was fast approaching one village when a big storm threatened. The natives had already taken refuge and shouted warnings. But I love the energy of a storm, the freshness it brings, and just kept on rolling. On the road earlier I had noticed people in stiff conical hats some three feet across which served as umbrellas if no friendly roof was available. Now I understood.

Just as the full fury of the storm hit, the back tire punctured for my first flat since the Nullarbor. Half rolling, half carrying Maria, I trudged on through blinding sheets of rain until I reached an unoccupied thatch roof. The rain stopped as suddenly as it started. I made my patch, carefully studied by the villagers who gathered from all over the hillsides. I was a novelty. My skin was white.

Typical rush hour traffic on a main street of Jogjakarta, Java

Feeling hungry, I was directed to the only eating house within miles. It offered tea and bananas, bananas and tea, nothing more. I paid seven cents for fourteen of the best bananas I've eaten. Altogether, I ate thirty-six bananas that day, slightly more than my usual daily average.

In Java bananas come in all sizes and shapes, from finger length to fifteen inches long and three inches across, sometimes round, elliptical, even square, sometimes red, golden, yellow, or green, sometimes firm, mushy or even crunchy. Whatever the size, shape or color, they are invariably delicious.

The road was now much slicker. It dropped down another lumpy rockpile, arched across a bridge over a raging stream, climbed a few more kilometers to the next village, where it stopped, stopped dead. My heart sank. But I did find an old track. A sign warned about its use, it was blocked to prevent any vehicle bigger than a bicycle from getting through. Down I went, down, down, down, slipping and sliding, falling, clinging to the steep side, avoiding the long drop. There were no people, no cultivation.

Everything is more beautiful, more meaningful, more interrelated, more natural, when one travels—like a wild animal—without security. The night? Let it fall. Tiger? Let it come. Storm? Let it begin. I don't much care. I was living my dream, filling my memory, stretching my limits.

Later, happily cycling through the small village of Peninggaran, a well-dressed man waved me down. He spoke a little English. Would I like some tea and bananas, and where would I spend the night? He laughed when I said I would stay in the nearest hotel. "That's a full day's ride away. Best you stay here." His name was Pawirosentono, and he was very cultured despite his isolation. I had to use my best manners. I had to remember to touch my chest after shaking hands, remember to leave food on my plate to show that there had been enough, remember to belch loudly to show that I had enjoyed the meal, remember to touch no food with my left hand. (In Asia the left hand is used in lieu of toilet paper. I heard of a man killed in Afghanistan for offering a loaf of bread with his left hand.)

On ahead the road became even rougher, the rocks even slicker. Again I walked more than I rode. Men by the hundreds were digging ditches beside the road with primitive tools. They stood in reverent silence, mouths agape, betel juice oozing down their chins, as I passed, smiling and nodding at each one.

In Pekalongan I visited in the home of Budiman, father of Budiharso. I was treated to a betjek tour of the city and given a beautiful batik shirt. One of the brothers even fixed my bike's twisted and rusted derailleur.

But perhaps the greatest thing about my stay was the eating. Breakfast included pork brains boiled to remain whole, sliced tongue and salted eggs, all on rice, of course. The salted eggs take ten days to "cook." A mixture of salt, saltpeter, and ground-up bricks, with enough water to form a mudpack, is placed around the egg. The result tastes nothing at all like an egg or anything else describable. It was good, I think, although it went down fast, very fast.

I ate barbecued goat, lamb soup, including stomach, intestines and testicles, and bamboo shoots. For desert we had a durien, a fruit covered with sharp spikes. It stinks like something rotten but tastes wonderfully good provided you pinch your nose.

From Pekalongan to Jakarta the road was flat and hot and crowded. The loads carried on bicycles and betjeks amazed me. In one betjek sat a man with two goats, another carried a woman perched high on a load of onions. One bike carried at least 500 pounds of huge clay pots, another was so burdened with a load of chairs I couldn't see the rider.

When I reached Tjierebon, the intense early-afternoon heat forced me to stop at the first hotel. A late meal in the heart of the city meant a ride back across town in the dark. On that dark ride I noticed that none of the other bicycles, betjeks, or carts had lights or reflectors. The next morning, under a nearly full moon, I joined the nocturnal confusion of black, slow-moving silhouettes. It was tricky avoiding other vehicles, railway lines, and horse droppings, and reading road signs was next to impossible, but I never felt in danger.

Next morning I started for Jakarta now only forty miles away two hours before dawn. Even that early, traffic was crowded. I suspect I wouldn't have lasted long in similar conditions in America, but, in Java, the drivers of the big trucks and buses are used to watching for slow, unlit vehicles, blowing their horns a lot, always stopping short of slaughter.

At the Australian High Commission in Jakarta I received my first mail in two months: twenty-eight letters, one package. I saw the package cost $61.00 to send by air mail.

It was from John Turner of John's Cyclery in St. Albans, West Virginia. I hadn't ever met John. He had read in one of my articles about my wish for a lower gear. He sent a complete conversion kit to make Maria a fifteen-speed bicycle, along with a new chain, new sprockets, new cables, new derailleurs, new crank, and other extras. Suddenly, the mountains of Sumatra did not sound so big.

Typical highway traffic throughout much of Java

At the youth hostel in Jakarta I exchanged stories with other Western travelers. More than half of those I talked with had been robbed in Indonesia. One man had been robbed twice and almost a third time in the same day. I think I escaped the thieves by looking poor, which was no pose, keeping my camera hidden, and being overly cautious in tourist areas.

Finally, I rode the last eleven miles in heavy traffic to the port to catch the cruise ship *Le Havre Abeto*, the Java journey finished, over, done with. Some Balinese had reckoned I had little chance of getting through alive. Well, there I was, alive and well, and heading for Sumatra.

My intinerary would take me into big mountains, covered by jungle, straddling the equator, the home of tigers, elephants, orangutans, snakes. The population would be sparse, monsoons could hit at any time. Sumatra thrummed with promise—and I was impatient to wrap myself in those mountains.

Chapter 10

Sumatra

A funny thing happened to me on my way to Padang in Sumatra. During a two-day cruise, which was otherwise pleasant and restful, especially with the seas not running very high, I had what amounted to a brand new experience. Despite a cast-iron digestive tract conditioned to virtually anything, I ran into some food I simply couldn't ingest.

Breakfast aboard the ship wasn't all that bad, although the egg was fried to a knot and served on top of the standard bowl of rice. But lunch was quite another matter. The rice looked no different, of course, same as anywhere else through the Asian land mass, except for one thing. The entree riding the top of the rice was a fish head, fairly large, ominous, almost blinking at me, badly undercooked, if the chef had even bothered putting it in a skillet at all. In the circumstances, I made other plans for lunch, such as no lunch at all.

By the time we gathered in the galley for dinner I had worked up such an appetite I might have qualified for the finals of the pie-eating contest at the county fair. Mercifully, what lay before me on the table looked wildly promising, a great bowl of rice, what else, along with a generous roast done to exactly the shade I liked.

Operating only with a fork and spoon, which was all the instrumentation at hand, it wasn't surprising that I had trouble cutting through the roast. When the cook noticed my problem, he kindly fetched a knife, a fairly sharp knife, too, although no more effective than the spoon no matter how energetically I sawed, stabbed, jabbed and ripped at the challenge before me. In the end I was forced to pick it up off the plate with my hands, family-style, and get a grip with my teeth. I chomped hard as I could, shaking the meat like a beagle trying to kill a rabbit, desperate to add some protein, before I surrendered because I could make little or no headway.

On retrieving my plate the cook couldn't help but notice the roast remained intact, humped on my chipped plate, defiant and triumphant. He obviously felt an explanation was in order.

"This buffalo very old," he said.

The ship cruised slowly into the harbor at Padang, scraping against the wharf, safely home from the sea. I was about to plunge into the unknown. I had seen no reference books, read no brochures, studied not even a large-scale map of Sumatra.

Leaving the ship, my bicycle fully loaded, the clock on the handlebar reading 20,917.0 miles, I merged into an outbound flow of people. But porters who had had a lifetime of experience swimming against the tide pushed and shoved as they returned again and again to unload cargo. After being battered in the human traffic jam for maybe fifteen minutes any instinctive sense of good manners evaporated. I used the bike as a club, trying to batter my way through the crowds, but I was hopelessly trapped until the police finally opened a lane and let me out.

If I had to lose something there in the harbor, however, better time than money. The only other American aboard the ship lost his bulging wallet in the melee.

First thing next morning I put the brand-new low gear on my bike to a ten-mile test up a steep mountain. It worked like a charm. Soon I was out in the bush country, in a tumble of mountains, the jungle a perfect fit all round me, wheeling free, with no particular destination in mind except for whatever sights lay on ahead. I felt a contentment I had seldom known.

The few small villages I passed included, along with dingy little houses, an occasional traditional house, circular, brightly painted, with pointed roofs rising to a peak at the top. On asking an elfish gentleman who showed me my room in a remote village named Solok, I was treated to the explanation—the legend—of why those dated shelters had pointed roofs, some with as many as six points.

Once upon a time Java told Sumatra that its people must become subjects of the Javanese kingdom. When Sumatra refused, Java threatened war before its rival pointed out that this was needless savagery. Instead of embarking on war, why not have a contest between prize bulls representing the two countries? Agreed.

Sumatra's leaders realized that even its very best bull was no match for the prize bulls from Java. What they did was take a bullock, sharpen its horns to a knife edge, and starve it for five days before the fight. Predictably, the bull bull from Java lost its competitive fury when it saw its opponent was only half-grown. Predictably too, the hungry bullock saw some dim resemblance to its mother in the rival, mostly because of equivalent size, and, rushing to where the udder ought to have been hung, fatally jabbed its sharpened horns into its side. A number of pointed house roofs, designed to express a symbolic appreciation of the bullock, have lived in Sumatra ever afterwards.

Traditional house near Solok, Sumatra, Indonesia

The next few days rolled up a patchwork of impressions. I rode by a succession of mosques each built to a different design, crossed a saddle between two active volcanoes, skirted the edge of a lake that stretched for more than ten miles. Where the jungle hadn't swallowed up the land, fields lay beautifully tended, looking almost lacquered on the green green countryside.

By nature I enjoy open spaces far more than crowds. This personal preference applied especially in Sumatra, where the country was stunning beyond any singing of it, the cities dirty and awash with foul odors. The people themselves were essentially kind, friendlier than the Balinese or Javanese, mostly basic and with no formal education, except for a surprising curiosity whose banal sameness eventually drove me straight up the wall.

"Hello, mister," people in every town would say. "Where do you go? Where are you from? What is your name?"

The repetition varied only if the natives had a slightly greater command of English. Then the volley was enlarged with three more questions.

"What is your age?" any advanced students invariably asked. "Are you married? Why not?"

During my 597 miles in Sumatra I was greeted with something more than that on only two occasions. A grown man walking toward me came to a stop, sucked in a deep breath and, grandstanding his abilities as a linguist, offered up a topical news bulletin: "To center of town today I go." Another adult solemnly greeted me with a personal admission: "I no make decision now."

After passing through the Panti jungle I wheeled a free bed in the jailhouse in tiny Muara Cubadak, where the resident policeman sponsored a bath in a small creek out behind, a generous bowl of chili so spicy my eyes began to water, friendly conversation on the front steps with a procession of resident girls in their most colorful clothes parading past to check out the stranger in town.

"You like one marry?" The policeman lifted his voice enough for the girls to hear. "Make good wife."

"No, I have no room on my bicycle for a wife," I told him.

"Ho, ho," he announced at roughly the same decibel count. "He say bicycle his wife."

But after I fell asleep that decent policeman stayed up right through the night copying from my English/Indonesian dictionary—an admirable effort at self-improvement. In the morning he gave me a breakfast of goat's milk, bread and some firm advice.

"Road climb in jungle," he said. "No village. Many tigers still hunting. Eat you up. Big sure."

"Could be." It was not the last I was to hear of tigers. "But if they do, you can have my dictionary and the bicycle."

On the basis of fairly extensive reading I seriously doubted that he would inherit either one, of course. Like other animals, tigers prefer to leave people alone unless they are provoked, and I had no plans to provoke any tigers I happened to encounter. It is perfectly true that a few people are killed every year, but the odds of becoming tiger fodder are so slim that I suspect a ride through the jungle at night is safer than a nocturnal stroll through many a big city.

"Why built on stilts?" The weathered old man in Samosir couldn't quite get a grip on my question. "Why houses built on stilts?"

It had struck me as a perfectly reasonable question. After all, the picturesque little houses rising to pointy saddle-shaped roofs arched up a hillside, a fairly steep hillside, in fact, where even the heaviest rain couldn't flood them. Yet a twine of wooden stilts lifted every one of the houses a few feet up off the green grassy land. Why?

"Tigers." Once he understood the question, the old man seemed bewildered that I couldn't guess at the answer. "Tigers, they don't climb ladders."

Every so often that matter-of-fact explanation cast a shadow over the sunshine of the day as I wheeled an empty roadway toward the Sibiayak volcano. Riding the slopes through a bamboo forest, the tires singing in the quiet, a whisper of breeze fanning me enough to diminish the heat, I experienced that euphoria all over again. Up there in the mountains the world no longer seemed out of joint.

For a while I even had some pleasant company, a ragamuffin boy, not over seven years old, quick, dark-eyed, smiling, improbably smoking a cigarette, who was riding a full-grown bicycle by sticking one leg through the frame to reach the other pedal. We climbed together, covering a mile or so. I won a challenge race easily, of course, and explained—here beginneth the lesson—that it wasn't because of my years or my longer legs, but because as a non-smoker I had stronger lungs. The boy, nodding seriously, promptly used the stub of his cigarette to light another. So much for unsolicited advice.

Soon I was beyond such signs of civilization as the boy on the bike. Soon the track up the mountain tilted to an angle I couldn't comfortably ride myself. I hid Maria in a clump of bamboo, stuffed what I needed in a small packsack, set out for the rim afoot, feeling very

The house on stilts where I stayed on the island of Samosir, Sumatra

At Kabund Jahe, Sumatra, I met a boy whose father told him he could start smoking when he could ride a man's bicycle.

much at peace with myself despite the hazards what few natives I had
seen had warned me about.

"We go up the mountain only when it is necessary—and sometimes
not even then," one of them had said. "It is better you not go yourself."

As he and several others told me, the reason they avoided the climb
was the fear of tiger or leopard, two great cats prevalent throughout
the island, especially in the high country where the number of humans
thins out. An elderly woman went so far as to plead with me to avoid
the ascent. In an effort to dissuade me she cited specific chapter and
verse—a tiger ripping two natives apart in this spot, for one, a leopard
clawing a bamboo farmer to death here, for another.

Certainly the ledger for the year before wasn't all that encouraging:
forty-three dead, nobody knew exactly how many injured, by tigers.

Whatever the moderate degree of risk, however, I was determined
to continue my climb. I had traveled too many miles, too many months
to miss filing a sightsee like Sibiayak away in my memory. Besides,
the great cats traditionally did their hunting at night and, unless
things went badly, I would safely be back down the mountain long
before dusk.

So up I went, moving fairly fast, picking my way along a track
through the forest, up, up, up. It was quiet, quiet and peaceful, and
the day lay sunny and warm around me. I paused for a brief snack,
rejoicing in my isolation, although still dimly aware of the perils out
there beyond me.

Back home in America, an eminent business mogul accustomed to
addressing large audiences used to start his standard speech with a
story about a New Yorker who packed off to the Far East for a tiger
hunt.

"Well, how many did you shoot?" a friend asked on his return.

"None."

"Too bad."

"Not really. When you're out after tigers none is plenty."

Those were my sentiments as I climbed toward the crater. None
would be plenty. Near the top the volcano roared, spewing steam and
sulphur fumes like a dragon, a fireburst, an awesome thing, something I won't ever forget. Was this particular trip necessary? You bet
your life it was.

During the night rain had sheeted down for a long while. A slick
coating of mud on the trail was soft and smooth. Most of it was
smooth, anyway. On my way back down I came to a jarring stop.
Before me a pattern of tracks that hadn't been there on my way up
appeared in the fresh mud. They were the tracks of some cat, a very

big cat, no doubt about it, prints laid down in the soft goo, menacing to a point where my scalp throbbed. Even worse, they pointed up the mountain, which meant that it was now somewhere behind me.

I stiffened, listening hard as I could. In the thick spread of the jungle I tried to detect a rustle of movement. Nothing. I took a soft step. Was that a faint noise behind me? Maybe, maybe not. I couldn't be sure. My nerve ends stretched tight as a drum, and I tried to reassure myself with the touchstone that tigers and leopards attack only at night—or so I thought.

Given that shock and alarm, my senses opened like a radar screen to register the nearby sights and sounds. I saw bamboo clumps, staghorn plants and banana trees, I heard the wooden call of a bird, I

A fluted tree in Sumatra

smelled the sweet, faintly musky odor of the jungle. Slowly, very slowly, I turned all the way around. The prints led up the trail, a rising beat of fear, disappeared in the edge of the forest.

Stepping carefully, I trundled on down the mountain in hopes I would make it. I spun at every alien sound, searching for safe shelter in case I needed it. But the sinewy attack I expected never came. At the bottom I collected my bike and twirled off as fast as I could go.

Today I nourish some schizoid feelings about my experience. I was relieved that whatever beast left that spoor—a look at a reference book on animal tracks unmistakably showed it to be a leopard later—hadn't come back out of the forest, of course, and yet I was strangely disappointed that time ran out without at least a glimpse. How I would have loved the thrill of sighting—at a distance, understand—the cat that quite plainly had followed me most of the way up the mountain without ever making a meal of me.

On my way to Lake Manindjau I stopped at the magical, time-haunted village of Bukittinggi. Among other local customs, the social structure is matriarchal, with the oldest woman in a family the absolute monarch. In case a man decides he wants to marry he must ask permission not only of the girl's mother but also of her grandmother—and he must agree to support his wife's sisters before even his own sons, if it ever comes to that.

For the sake of novelty I caught a bus on a side trip to Manindjau. Some novelty! It was licensed to carry a legal load of no more than 24 passengers. By actual count 56 people and a live chicken crowded onto our bus. I'm still not sure how so many people could breathe in so cramped a space, although, personally, I breathed a bit less than I was accustomed to.

After we finally reached our destination—the bus broke down three different times the first mile, crawled up a hill with such ennui that I got out and walked—I hiked to the rim of an extinct crater. Butterflies, cloudbursts of butterflies, filled the air along the shores of the deep blue lake half a mile below. They came in assorted sizes and colors, flutters of yellow, blue, green, orange, red, brown, even black, some no larger than hominy grits, others big as birds.

Although it took me a few moments, I saw something indigenous besides butterflies at Lake Manindjau, too. A thin little man, all vertical lines and bulging eyeballs, angrily cursed and shook his fist at the top of a coconut tree. Overtrained, I thought, badly overtrained, perhaps even loony. Then my eyes tracked a rope stretched from his bony hand up to a plump monkey playing truant in the fronds high at the top of the tree. After blinking at the reward of a big banana his co-worker the man frantically waved down below, the monkey went into his normal routine, twisting ripe coconuts off the tree, dropping them to the ground.

"A good working monkey can pick around seven hundred coconuts a day," a passerby who observed the strained labor relations told me.

As things turned out, I didn't ride that hellish crowded bus back to Bukittinggi. As things turned out, I rode no bus at all. The last one had left hours before, which meant that I faced up to my first Sumatran hitch. It couldn't have been easier. Every single driver who came past—even a motorcycle without the power to climb a hill with two riders—offered me a lift. An Army jeep took me around the forty-four switchback turns to escape the crater.

A day later I spun Maria through rolling land dim with distance reaching for the equator. As a bustling local tourist attraction, the magical line generally had a crowd on hand to greet the traffic from either direction. After twenty eventful months "down under" I was crossing back into the northern hemisphere.

On a hot sweltering night in Padangsidinguan at the end of ninety-four wearying miles on the bike my temper boiled over. It wasn't so much because the town was dirty, foul smells rising in the sticky air, although that was part of it. It wasn't so much because residents insisted on swarming around the bike, trying the brakes, ringing the bell, switching the gear levers, although that was part of it, too.

It wasn't even because the hateful old music sounded again: Hello, mister. Where do you go? What is your name? Hello, mister, hello, mister, hello, mister . . .

On sorting the experience out in my mind later I realized that it was a combination of all these elements, plus the fact that I was back in an urban arena after several days in the open by myself. Wherever I traveled on my long pull round the world, whatever the language, cities invariably sunk me in a mild despair. Perhaps because of my lifelong fondness for the outdoors, my good spirits are dampened by the clutter, the traffic, the noise, the stench of anything much bigger than a village. At the risk of paraphrasing Goldsmith, I generally find cities to be places where people accumulate and wealth decays.

No matter what series of events contributed to it, the sight of one more Sumatran boy jeopardizing the cables on the bike by moving the gear levers provoked a memorable rage. I screamed. I screamed so hard I could see people stop in their tracks a block away. I screamed so hard the sound of it was painful even to me. Oddly, it struck me at the time that I hadn't screamed at anyone ever before.

In the relative quiet of my hotel room later that night I couldn't help but try to understand my reactions. If the people here expressed a lively curiosity about who I was, where I was going, where I came from, if they expressed a personal interest in the bike I was riding, if

A crowd was on hand to welcome Maria and her rider back to the northern hemisphere, at the equator in Sumatra.

they persisted despite my warnings, they were little or no different from other individuals in other lands who had behaved in much the same manner. I decided it was a matter of dramatic contrasts. One moment I was up in the hills by myself, the next moment I was locked in the crowd of a city. If and when my trek finally came to an end, I would resolve the matter of contrasts by opting out and becoming a practicing hermit.

Things started no better early the next day. While I settled my modest bill the hotel clerk informed me that tigers had killed a total of nine people in the general area. Before I could get to my bicycle, someone gave the bell an insistent ring. Overreactive, still feeling an emotional hangover from the night before, I screamed again.

Even out in the healing slopes of Sumatra it looked as if there was no escape. On catching sight of me a young boy twining along on a bike slowed down, rode alongside me for an impromptu conversation. But his questions were thoughtful and went right to the bone. How would Nixon's resignation affect U.S. policy abroad? Had I heard the latest news from Cyprus? Would population control actually save the world from starvation? As the miles spun by I felt better and better.

The track I happened to be riding that day assayed more pedestrians than traffic. They used it for sitting, napping, strolling, even playing cards. I rang my bell frequently and rode on, the pressures of the previous night unwinding all the time.

In Sibolga I won one, lost one. The hotel made me pay extra for tea, which came as a surprise, but a restaurant right next door served something more than rice-based food, up to and including ice cream, genuine ice cream, so good I called for another round. Sleep wasn't all it might have been, not with a loud game of dominos in the room below, with light leaking through some holes in the wall, and a mattress with broken springs coiling up into it, but the sleep was sufficient for my purposes.

My informal tour of Sumatra stretched wherever I chose. I cycled past herds of swaybacked pigs, rolled down into yawning valleys, saw endless shades of green climbing toward waterfalls, dramatic mountains and jungle. Along the way I came upon sights I might never see again, experiences to warm me through the long winters when I got home again.

In Belige a student who was all of eighteen carefully outlined the firm long-range program he had assigned himself. He had chosen his future bride, whom he would marry exactly eleven years hence. Meanwhile, they couldn't go out together alone, must be seen only in crowds and couldn't so much as talk together at any length, else he would become an object of ridicule on the basis of local custom.

In Pangururan an attractive young native girl named Dyana, who spoke surprisingly good English, didn't so much as blush in articulating her hopes for the future. She was determined to marry soon. What's more, she was determined to marry a stranger. Quite plainly, someone who'd ridden a bicycle from a home base more than half a world away fit the specifications.

"Do you know that Indonesian girls make good wives to strangers?" The preliminary windup inevitably led to the high hard one. "Would you like to marry an Indonesian girl?"

At the risk of offending a pleasant young girl, I told her that I couldn't possibly contemplate such permanent moorings until I completed my global trek a year or so later. She seemed to understand from past experiences. As she explained it, only one or two Europeans came through the village every week, and, while she always put the big question—not very flattering to me, I thought—to those fellow wanderers, she had yet to receive a favorable playback. At the moment she was saving her money to move to Panang, where the prospects ought to be better. I hope they were.

On an alarmingly steep four-mile ascent beyond Harrangoal I didn't have to shift down into my splendid new low gear. Laughing and shouting, several friendly young boys took turns pushing me up the sharp slope. The mountain may or may not have come to Mohammed, but that particular one came comfortably to me.

On scenic Samosir I found a cook accustomed to catering to Western tastes. For breakfast I had a banana pancake, for example, thick as a beefsteak, ten inches across, heaped with banana, pineapple, papaya and other fruits, the whole of it topped with grated coconut, chocolate and whipped cream, total cost $.12. Other dishes were equally toothsome, equally cheap. Despite my voracious appetite, I couldn't manage to eat a dollar's worth of food the day I tried my best.

In view of skyrocketing food prices elsewhere around the world, in view of the peace, the calm, the weather, even the mountains, a stray thought rose in my mind. Why not stay here? The land had a beauty to it, the streams, the lakes, the air were pure, that abundance of food could be had at incredibly low prices. Why not blinking well stay on Samosir?

Well, I did stay. I didn't stay forever, of course, despite the temptation. But I was so caught in the spell that I stayed for a few more days. Then I remembered that other yearning dreamlands—Nepal and Kenya, South Africa and Britain—still lay before me.

On my very last day I noticed a flow of blood when I crossed my legs relaxing over a cold drink. A close examination revealed a small round hole just above my sock, the mark of a leech, a leech which had sucked its fill back in the bush and dropped off somewhere. It seemed appropriate. The jungle had taken a last incidental bite out of me.

In Medan I learned that a ship was leaving for Penang in Malaysia that same night. I rode twenty-four miles to the port flat-out, pumping fast as I could, weaving in traffic, soaked in sweat. A quick ticket, random customs clearance, a sprint up the gangplank and an especially fascinating leg of my two-wheeler trek was over and done with. I had done something more than survive it. I had enjoyed it to a point where it ached some to leave.

Chapter 11

Malay Peninsula

Someone who obviously knew his way around the globe once remarked that Penang in the Malay Peninsula offered the best of both worlds. Personally, I wouldn't quarrel with that view. The food was even better than in Indonesia, and every bit as cheap, accurate maps and other basic materials were available, the people themselves were warm, friendly and considerate.

My introduction to Butterworth after an easy crossing to the mainland seemed wildly promising. It wasn't merely the fact that a comfortable and commodious room I booked over a Chinese restaurant came to only $1.25. But the facilities also included a luxury I had almost forgotten wheeling through other lands in the same general latitudes: toilet paper.

I rode south toward Singapore straight into the clatter of thick traffic and monsoons such as I hadn't experienced in Sumatra. The rain came down in great sheets, stiff, blinding, almost a wall of rain. Unable to ride in the deluge I joined other cyclists and motorcycle buffs under the nearest overhang of roof. But generally the rain stopped as abruptly as it began. We rode in sunshine for half an hour or so, sought refuge when the monsoon let go again, and carried on through an endless sequence of sunlight and downpours like trick bulbs on a Christmas tree, until I finally arrived in Kuala Kangsar.

During a sightsee ride through town I came upon a mosque so lovely that I shot up a full roll of film. A golden onion-shaped central dome, still wet from the hard rains, caught the last rays of sun as another storm cloud rolled up behind. Surrounded by green lawns and majestic coconut palms, the mosque rose over the land, slim and perfect, an arrangement of twenty-four other smaller domes, towers and spires giving it an even greater beauty than the Taj Mahal, in my opinion. And it was serendipitous, too, something I hadn't expected or heard of, which made it even more pleasurable.

At the hotel there in Kuala Kangsar the owner took a pragmatic approach when I asked him about an alternate route on to Singapore. Along with several other natives who joined in the conversation, he strongly urged me to stick to the main highway even though it hummed with traffic. The only other route ran through the jungle, where the traffic, while predictably thinner, consisted more of hazards like man-eating tigers, which everyone assured me had a hellish taste for Americans as well as Orientals.

Next morning I cycled into the jungle, not out of any latent death wish, far from it, in fact, but simply because I felt the perils of a major highway were greater than the jungle. One man's five-ton lorry is another man's tiger.

For forty miles the track unwound like a cyclist's daydream. Shaded, with few S-turns, most of it fairly flat, it ran along the river until it simply disappeared. My map showed a brief gap, another connecting track not far away. Yet on asking a friendly resident, I learned that it wasn't as easy as the map indicated.

"Yes, you can go through." A bent man with a pennywhistle beard, small, dressed in sandals and a dirty kimono, he eyed me with a look of consternation. "But many crossroads, no signs, rough, many rock, many mud, many high grass. You have good sense, go back. You have crazy head, go on."

In case he had entertained any doubts, they evaporated once he saw me push on ahead. Rocks gave way to dirt, wet with slick, the track narrowed to a single bicycle lane, the whole of the jungle closed in around me. Still, the marks of other bikes ran on before me and, besides, I'd ridden the Nullarbor and Samosir, hadn't I?

Before long, however, it was apparent that my logic was no better than the route I had chosen. Both were potted with holes. Even those reassuring tracks didn't mean much. It was true that there were bicycles on ahead, loaded down with bananas, but they were being pushed, not ridden, and I learned they didn't cover the perplexing gap on my map. The more I advanced, the more ominous things looked.

Lashing monsoon rains had turned the narrow six-inch path into mud pie; sharp grass rose like cactus on either side. Any time I came upon a minor junction I was forced to navigate by wild intuition. When I cryptically shouted "Telok Anson?" at a native, his dark eyebrows arched to register shock at my destination.

By midday scudding clouds visible up through the thick vegetation darkened. In a matter of minutes the rains began, heavy, very heavy, wetting me right to the bone, and there was no roof for shelter. I spun as hard as I could, reaching for a track that couldn't be that far off, provided the map was accurate, or the jungle hadn't blotted it out, or it led where I was aiming.

The mosque at Kuala Kangsar, Malaysia

Fellow "road" users on the jungle track between Kuala Kangsar and Telok Anson, Malaysia. During the entire world trip Maria had only six wrecks; three of those were on this track.

In a global spin that currently read 22,234.5 miles on the odometer I had fallen off Maria only twice before, once in Oklahoma, back when I was fairly new at the game, and a second time in Sydney, where it wasn't really my fault. But in the thick of the Malaysian jungle, riding the full blast of a monsoon, traveling a wet lane fenced in by grass, I fell a total of three times.

Just as I began to despair the verdancy opened slightly into a gravel road. A native in a red slicker sprinted out of a nearby house to warn me that I was on a private estate.

"May I ride it?" I asked.

"Yes." He paused briefly. "But come, please, sit awhile."

His teen-age wife—the man in the slicker must have been on the sunny side of 40—shyly served cakes and a glass of hot cocoa, although I noticed that neither one joined me.

"This is Ramadan," he explained. "Moslems cannot eat, drink or smoke between sunrise and sunset this month."

"Don't you get hungry during the day?"

"No, not much. We have a big feast before sunrise."

That was something I could understand. I hadn't been eating on a three-a-day schedule myself. But something more than the religious dietary strictures intrigued me.

"How is the road ahead?"

"Um." The look on his face wasn't encouraging. "For a bicycle, I think, very bad."

And so it was. After the next torrential stage of the recurring monsoon absolutely the worst cycling conditions of my global spin commenced. Every few yards I was forced to dismount, scoop handfuls of mud off the tires, the fork, the brakes. Pushing Maria in the grass beside the path, I went too near the edge, tumbling hard down a steep bank, the bike pinning my left leg, a mudslide threatening to bury both of us until I caught hold of a tree.

After wiping the bike and wiping enough goo off my face to see some, I switched into super low gear and slowly rode a ten-inch ditch filled with water. It wasn't fast, of course, but at least the water wiped the wheels clean while I worked the pedals.

Late that afternoon, while I was moving along at greater speed, the track came to an end. It disappeared just like that, bang, now you see it, now you don't, up against a river bank, with nothing showing either left or right. It seemed so tragic that I whooped with laughter. There I was, lost, soaked in mud, too worn down to cycle back through the jungle, doomed to spend the night in the wet. I didn't exactly relax and enjoy it, as the old joke goes, but I relaxed to the extent I could, stretching on the wet ground, arms and legs in a sprawl.

"You like go Telok Anson, my boat?"

Magically a boy appeared, a small boy, raggedy, smiling, offering me a ride in the motorboat tied to a pier beyond a roll of grass. As his father swung the boat upriver the boy washed the mud off my bike, and I dangled over the stern doing what I could to clean myself.

Not up to searching for a cheap hotel in Telok Anson, not up to much of anything, really, I aimed straight for the police station for a room. Ramli Arshad, the duty officer who treated me like a long-lost friend, kindly enlarged that to room and board.

"Hurry," he said. "It's six forty-three." Seeing I had gone blank, he interpreted. "The sun sets in four minutes. We must begin to eat when the fast ends."

At a restaurant not far away Ramli insisted on treating me to every one of the available foods I hadn't tried before, which was to say most of the menu. I was too tired to remember the names and tastes of the dishes we were served, but I remember one thing beyond a doubt.

Photo taken before the mud became too bad on the jungle track in Malaysia

They were all of them wonderfully good. I left feeling bloated, satisfied. On our way back to the jailhouse the policeman offered me one last delicacy. He offered to get me a girl for the night.

In Singapore I took advantage of modern times. I bought a new camera and film, a spare tire, a book on the Thai language I would soon be tuning in, several beefsteaks thick as rib roasts. The guest house where I stayed even had a sit-down toilet. After a lapse of months I found it awkward and uncomfortable compared to the fundamental Eastern squat.

The variety and relative creature comforts of Singapore seemed abundant, especially after my recent trek through the rains, and so I sampled what I could. I almost sampled a traffic ticket for mistakenly cycling in a botanical garden too, except the policeman softened up when I went into a wheedling spiel in southern-flavored American.

But I could only take civilization in small doses. Whatever challenges lay awaiting me out in the backcountry, it was time to wheel off on the hot, twining road for Malaysia's enormous jungle national park at Taman Nagara. For the first time since Australia I pitched my tent, rolled inside for a wooly nap.

A park ranger taught me a few basic words of the local dialect as I dined at his invitation on a meal too hotly seasoned to finish. The ranger's wife was hotter still. Although neither seemed very concerned, she was delirious with malaria. Personally, I hoped the bitter pills I had been taking for several weeks would be worth the gag factor.

Small huts nestled among the trees, water buffalo grazed open land, mountains rose up ahead during a hitch on a 60-foot motorboat with a ridiculously narrow four-foot beam. We carried lumber, food, a chest of drawers and, oddly, a child's rocking horse for river people along the way.

At the end of the ride another ranger suggested that I set out afoot for an animal "hide" twelve miles away. With any luck I might see elephant, tiger, tapir and even black panther visiting a salt lick. Three young women from Switzerland joined me for the trip. We carried our own food—and there were beds to spend the night at the hide.

The four of us hadn't walked a crooked trail for more than 100 yards before some local wildlife caught hold of me. It was a leech, a blood leech, bothersome but not painful. Another leech glued itself on slender, fair-haired Carmen's neck, two more bored into my left foot, all of them curling and dropping when I used a match flame.

But the floor of the forest was literally paved with leeches. Soon the four of us had attracted so many that it was futile to waste time with matches. We buttoned, unbuttoned, yanked them off, paused at every stream to wash the blood away. The resident leeches were not observing Ramadan. Unfortunately, the normal demands of nature had to be answered every so often too, which exposed a tender pink bottom to the ever hungry leeches.

Troops of monkeys swung through the foliage around us, chattering, skinning their stained teeth, pictures out of old Tarzan movies. They were a pleasure to see swinging from vine to vine, and we toddled along swiveling our necks up and down, up and down, looking for leeches at our feet, looking for monkeys in the trees, which wasn't so bad, except for one thing.

Any time a person confines his vision to a vertical plane he's apt to neglect the horizontal, as I abruptly did in those circumstances. A small snuffling sound rose, amplified to a snort, and a big bull boar, his six-inch tusks glistening in the speckled light, charged me from off to our right. I leaped for a low branch, pulled myself up as the tusks fanned the air just below. Lucky, I told myself, extremely lucky.

I dropped to the ground after he passed, a thin ooze of sweat covering me, and the boar, quick, agile as a cat, charged again. I used the branch to escape a second time, heard the three terrified girls scream when he stopped between us, quivering, pawing the matted grass. Finally the beast backed off to rejoin the herd, and my blood pressure backed off to something approaching normal.

We watched the salt lick from two in the afternoon until darkness closed in at seven without seeing anything more than a small otter. We slept under mosquito netting on comfortable mattresses, which were luxury items in many a city I had recently toured. And once my three companions from Switzerland stopped giggling we heard the music of the night, eerie and strange, coughs, hacks, baying, anonymous noises we couldn't quite identify out beyond us. If we hadn't seen any major animals except for the boar, at least we were hearing them in some profusion.

Later, days later, I would gladly have settled for a distant sound instead of a close-up confrontation.

Little things kept going wrong in the Malaysian backcountry. By themselves they didn't amount to much, not in a long-view sort of way, but together they hammered at my sunny disposition. I'm not superstitious by nature, but I ought to have recognized the pattern for what it was.

On my way to Kuala Krai, for instance, I invested my last few remaining coins on my first food in a full day, fifteen bananas, fifteen green and bitter bananas, as things turned out, which I ate despite the taste, although I came to regret it when my belly coiled in knots cycling toward Thailand.

In scorching 95-degree humidity my rear tire went flat, not from a puncture, but from an old patch that literally melted off. In the village of Tanah Merah, after an especially hard day, my customary stop at the police station turned out badly. "Sorry, we take criminals only— no visitors," the constable told me.

On crossing the frontier into Thailand I found the roadway filled with miscellaneous traffic, bikes, motorbikes, motorcycles, cars, trucks and lorries, even malevolent columns of military vehicles. Pinned in the backwash of war, a procession of more than 200 trucks and tanks, machine guns bristling from the backs of the trucks, drove a number of natives off the road and into safe shelter in the trees.

The sun beat down without pause, locked in a clear sky, with no sign of a healing rain. It beat down so hard that several other patches on my tubes came unglued, which meant I had to make frequent stops along the way, roughing the surface, spreading more stickum, hoping the new patches would hold for a few miles. The sun beat down so hard it finally raised a painful blister on my lower lip. For the first time since way back in Lynchburg, Virginia, for the first time since my round-the-world spin began, I seriously wondered whether it was worth carrying on.

In Naroothiwat, a sweltering village teetering on the rim of my memory, a repairman sadly shook his head. The loose spokes on my bike couldn't be tightened. They had rusted into place.

On the edge of town, bound for Bangkok by way of a series of settlements whose beauty I couldn't properly appreciate with things going so badly, several Buddhists raised two specific warning flags for me. The road ahead was littered with guerrillas, who slipped out of the jungle to rob, maim and even kill, guerrillas and elephants. Just recently a work elephant gone berserk had grabbed a man by the leg and beaten him to death against a tree.

Yet there were some compensations for my assorted miseries, too. The people themselves were unfailingly kind, courteous, incredibly gentle, the very friendliest people I was to encounter anywhere. A shopkeeper once chased me down the street when I unknowingly paid too much for some food. In Pattani a Chinese lodgekeeper insisted there was no charge for a comfortable room.

In a remote lacquered-looking village named Haadyai I couldn't find accommodations anywhere until a young Buddhist monk invited me to stay at the temple. Like most of the young men in Thailand, he was serving as a monk only briefly, the better to learn humility and

Typical roadside cliffs in southern Thailand

other fundamental values of the faith. Clad in saffron robes, their heads shaved right down to the skin, my host and several others set out at dawn the next morning with brass begging bowls tucked under their arms.

For a few miles I thought the new day might be an improvement over my recent hard times. But my lower lip blistered in the heat haze, cracked, bled and blistered again. Just as I got to stretching over the distance another tire went flat, which was normal enough by now, although a wobbly wheel contributed to the flat. As I pumped the re-patched tire, the nozzle of my pump burst. Flinging the pump away, I called a recess by sitting down against a tree while my rage subsided. When the first ten or twelve inch-long red ants I inadvertently sat on simultaneously bit into me, up I went, rising like a rocket, before my head painfully banged against a limb.

If things couldn't possibly get any worse, they didn't get any better, to say the least.

Two work elephants, eight or ten feet at the shoulder, probably four tons each, walked with their mahouts on the road before me. It was a numbing sight, exotic and picturesque, a perfect picture of southern Thailand. Or at least it was until one of the elephants spooked at the sight of my bicycle and crashed off into the jungle with both mahouts chasing after him.

There I was, a stranger in a far-off land, alone with the other elephant whose intentions I had no way of assessing. The first thing he did was take a boisterous swipe at me with his trunk. It lashed in the heat, blowing my hat off, standing my hair on end. I levered into high gear, wheeled down the road as fast as I could. The big elephant followed along, trumpeting, his ears raised like sails, moving at more than twenty-five miles an hour.

During the shock of the chase I took to screaming at myself. Pump harder, legs, pump harder. Please, patches, don't come loose now. He was so close his trumpeting sounded amplified to a full decibel count.

A roll of hill loomed ahead of us. Faster, Maria, faster, faster. At the end of a mile the elephant was only thirty yards behind me. At the end of another mile he was visibly, audibly closing my perilous lead. A bittersweet thought came boiling to the surface of my mind: well, half a world adventure is better than none.

When the road rose again, just when my situation looked its absolute worst, the elephant stopped. I'm not sure exactly why he stopped with his target so close, although perhaps he was feeling the rigors of the race, same as I was, but I didn't much care. The elephant stopped

Enjoying a moment's respite from the scorching sun at a waterfall near Kra Buri, Thailand

dead in his great tracks and simply stood there bellowing while I kept wheeling the bike on ahead.

Once the worst of it was over and done with, an odd detachment came over me. The scene seemed distant, unreal, almost comical. At a prudent distance of a quarter of a mile or so I felt so detached that I even screwed the telephoto lens in place, turned for a picture. But he started up again, running, gathering speed, switching my detachment back to fear again.

I leaped onto the bike, the camera banging on my hand, and scattered some of my gear pumping away. I pumped hard for a mile, two miles, five miles, always hoping another patch wouldn't let go, and wound down some only when a long sweep of road behind showed nothing, nothing at all. But two hours later, and many a long mile down the road, I still apprehensively peered over my shoulder every so often in case this particular elephant had an aching memory for me.

She came strutting into my room without knocking, tall by local specifications, fairly attractive, peeled off most of her clothing. Then she demanded 200 baht, or approximately $10 U.S. Once again I had mistakenly checked into a brothel instead of a hotel.

Even if my poorboy budget allowed for such pleasures, I was too exhausted to perform. After all, I'd ridden eighty-six miles into Bangkok under a glassy sun that day, along a roller-coaster track, much of which wound past limestone caves, spectacular ferns and plant life, and monkeys squealing from vines, vivid scenes already rusting into memory.

Along with the sheer strain of the day I had experienced a bullying encounter with a motorcycle jock whose manners were emphatically non-Thailand. He jerked the flag off my bike, fitted it to his motorcycle. When I recovered the flag and walked my bike into a cafe, he followed.

"Thailand is the land of smiles—known world over," he said softly.

"So they tell me."

"You were angry with me just now."

"Yes. You took my flag."

"Thai people never steal."

"Oh."

But now I was confronted with this naked girl who shouted triumphantly to other sisters of the night as she banged the window shutters closed in the room. What to do, what to do?

"No, two hundred baht too much," I said. "One hundred baht."

In my fatigue I hadn't allowed for the universal professional flexi-

The elephant that chased me for over three miles in southern Thailand is here sufficiently tired to allow time to take this picture.

bility in the matter of negotiated rates. Slowly, the curves of her body undulating, she approached the bed.

"Okay," she said. "One hundred baht, okay."

"No, one hundred baht too much too." I set myself up and welched by fifty percent. "Fifty baht."

"One hundred baht, okay." She may still have been open to negotiations, of course, but she was momentarily locked in a holding pattern at 100 baht. "One hundred baht not too much."

To avoid any further conversation I showed the hopeful working girl that I had a total of no more than twenty-seven baht in cash, whereupon she dressed and stormed out of the room, trailing a storm-cloud of abuse.

Before I bedded down by myself I found that the room included a distinctive feature other brothels elsewhere built on piers might want to consider by way of providing cover for any suspect husbands. A hinged plank in the floorboards opened into the ocean, which meant a person could fish even without getting out of bed. A truant husband who wanted to tell his wife he had gone fishing could actually go fishing, simple as that, along with his other sport.

The next couple of days in Bangkok I ran an obstacle course of travel agents in a search for help. Overland travel across the hump of Burma was illegal, and so I had to push on to Nepal some other way. Like resident whores, travel agents had sliding scales, too. By shopping around I managed to save $55 on my ticket.

Criss-crossing the big urban sprawl I photographed several Buddhist temples, breath-taking architecture, some done in rainbow colors, all of them rising into fluted golden spires. One housed a magnificent Buddha composed of five and a half tons—that's right, *tons*—of solid gold.

On my last night thousands of people gathered at the waterway for the Loy Krathong festival. Everyone builds a float, generally on a banana leaf, decorates it with flowers, a small candle, sticks of incense and a small coin. Some are painfully elaborate, miniature temples and ships, swans and snakes. When the full moon rises over a tumble of trees the candles and incense are lighted and these krathongs are gently pushed into the lake as symbols of casting away the burdens of the year.

Since I had experienced recent troubles, I confected a krathong of my own, too, small, not especially ornamental, but in the proper spirit. Whatever there was to the ritual, my hopes soared, running up the scale to genuine contentment, when all the candles bobbed and flickered out across the lake in a bright sheen of moonlight.

Pedaling for the airport, I took an informal inventory of my tour of Thailand and Southeast Asia. Both Maria and I had come through pretty well. I'd been sick, painfully sick, only that day in Java. My bike had blown a number of tires without ever coming apart. I'd lost a hat but not my life to a rogue work elephant. The heat had been overwhelming, the sun almost more than I could bear, and yet I had survived. Besides, I had seen sights around the verdant corners of the jungle denied most people.

On balance then, I in no way regretted that arduous leg of my trip. Still, a flicker of excitement caught hold of me as I pushed on for another area, another culture, another land. And at least Nepal, rising high over the earth's surface, would be cooler.

Chapter 12

Nepal

"Tiger Tops Lodge is fabulous, fabulous." The man in Kathmandu, Nepal spoke in the glib hyperbolic tones endemic to sightsee vendors the world over. "You'll see rhinos for sure, probably leopard and, with any luck, a tiger. The package costs a mere $70 a day, including excellent meals."

It didn't sound like $70 a day, not with my economy flattened out, at least, but a trip to Tiger Tops in the Royal Chitwan National Park certainly sounded worth exploring. I explored with a modest restraint.

"Ten dollars a day," I said. "What about ten dollars a day for the full package?"

His eyeballs rolled agreeably. "Fine. You've just got time."

Within an hour I was airborne again, in a small plane filled with a global cast of tourists—how many of them had innocently accepted that opening bid of $70, I wondered—anxious to visit some wonders out in the raw. Manasalu, Annapurna, Dhaulagiri, other classic Himalayan peaks humped in the distance through the windows, savage, forbidding, capped with white snow.

Circling the airport during an easy descent, we watched men, women and children drive their cattle off the long grass runway. Since the luxury hotel the flimflam man back in Kathmandu had so lyrically described was served only from this remote airport, I guessed private cars would be awaiting us. The pilot, smiling at my innocence, pointed to the south. Our transportation was right on schedule—elephants, three elephants, swaying over the meadow, a mahout/chauffeur aboard each one.

The elephants knelt gently while eight of us clambered up, up into the wide wooden saddles complete with mattresslike cushions. The irony didn't escape me. It was a far better thing being on top of an elephant than a few fluctuating yards in front of one. Clutching the saddle, feeling the strength of the beast as it ponderously moved, we saw deer, peacock and smaller fowl in the thick grass along the trail.

The author rides an elephant native style at the Tiger Tops Lodge, Meghauli, Nepal. To reach his perch he had to grab an ear in each hand and walk up the trunk, foot over foot.

At a height of twelve feet or so I clicked off half a roll of color film before the most arresting shot of the ride appeared.

All of a sudden we heard a heavy rumbling sound. Then a one-horned Indian rhinoceros bolted into the clearing, braked to a stop, stood blinking at us. Two tons of evil, the rhino's long boat-shaped head, cobbled, armored hide and large horn curving to a point made it the perfect vision of doom. It stood still for a few moments, rumbling like a cannon, left only when our three elephants closed in from all sides.

As a park ranger explained later, this particular model of rhino, while making a modest comeback, was a species so endangered that not more than 100 still existed a few years before. As is all too often the case, the natural predator was man, who slaughtered the rhinos for the market value of some unique by-products. The horn was cut, powdered and sold as an aphrodisiac, which many orientals claim rejuvenates even the most inactive males. The bladder was squeezed dry of its urine, which was bagged and hung over native doorways to ward off disease and evil spirits.

The Tiger Tops Lodge was built on high stilts in a jungle clearing. By definition it was rustic, with no electricity, no motor noises, but it had a well-stocked bar and an enormous fireplace blazing in the middle of the lounge. It was pleasantly comfortable, especially after my own modest lodgings through most of Asia. In addition to everything else, for example, I wasn't accustomed to the splendid hired help/guest ratio. More than 100 employees catered to the whims of a maximum of 40 guests.

Soon after we began exploiting the various creature comforts to be had a cry went up from outside the lodge. A leopard had killed a goat nearby. We walked through the jungle barefoot for the sake of quiet, squeezed into a specially constructed blind. The leopard stood in a beam of spotlight, long and roped with muscle, a spotted length of menace, making snuffling noises while he fed on the carcass. The thought of the leopard that stalked me in Sumatra put a slight dent in my central nervous system.

I awakened next morning before I wanted. I awakened because all too many langur monkeys wouldn't let me sleep. Outside my window they set up a terrible din at first light, whooping as they swung through sal and rosewood trees, gray animals with coal-black faces, comical to watch even before the abundance of hired help padded to my doorway with a civilized cup of tea.

We saw other creatures great and small later that day. From an elephant we saw deer and peacock, another rhino, even another leopard, without going weak in the knees. An elephant down under a heavy saddle makes a marvelous security blanket.

Altogether we saw an assortment of game, more than our share, I suppose, but we didn't sight the one specimen we wanted to see most of all. In hopes of spotting the elusive tiger we went drifting downriver for ten miles by dugout canoe to a tent camp where prospects were said to be more promising. The hill country rose dramatically into the Himalayas off in the distance, while spindly white herons, all neck and legs, stood in the blue water against green bamboo shoots.

During our leisurely ride I saw a small black ball move through the river a few feet in front of our canoe. I made the proper connection. Crocodiles swim submerged except for their bulging eyes. It was a crocodile all right, and fairly big, half as long as the dugout, its body crusted with scales behind the flat throwback head. It swirled closer, straightened, fanned for the far bank.

At the wild outpost camp news was encouraging, if not guaranteed. While nobody had sighted a tiger for several weeks, conditions seemed about right to Bal Banadur Rai, the chief game scout. "It is absolutely necessary that the tiger come," Rai said. "I think at sunset."

Five of us ate dinner around a campfire in the dying day. Sunset came and went, the sky filled with stars. We probably talked more than we should have, in a desperate hope that the familiar old line of verse—"Tiger, tiger, burning bright/In the forests of the night"— would take shape in a blind half a mile away.

Out of the dark a native appeared, his bare feet drumming on the ground. He spoke softly with Rai, who reacted immediately.

"*Bag ayou.*" His voice was thinned to a whisper. "The tiger has come!"

We hurried through the jungle carrying no weapons. I suppose we might have come upon a leopard, a rhino, a local species of bear said to have especially short fuses, another tiger. We hurried through the night blotting out any sensations except for an urge to see the tiger.

Through peepholes in the brushy blind we waited for the big torch to switch on. A deer cried from somewhere close by. The torch lighted, scanned the area, focusing on a dead buffalo calf in the clearing, tracking down the bank, up a tree, over a fall in the land, up a second tree. But no tiger. After waiting for 15 minutes, half an hour, almost 45 minutes the guide sent us back to camp for some sleep.

Despondent, cursing my fate, I brewed another cup of tea and sat talking with others by the campfire. One of the longest shots in nature simply hadn't come up for us. Or so it seemed. But the guide came slipping through the trees with another bulletin: "The tiger is back. Come quickly."

We covered that dark half-mile as fast as we could run. After all the stops, all the distance, all the lands I had covered in Southeast Asia, there it was. Fixed in the light of the torch, standing over the dead buffalo, his smooth, golden-orange neck arched to the left, the royal Bengal tiger was big, big as they come, according to the guide, well over 500 pounds. He paused and sniffed at the soft wind, the striped body coiled, skittish and distracted.

The experience was overwhelming for me. The memory lingers still, the memory and an incidental thought. I had seen a tiger in the bush without the tiger ever seeing me, which is far and away the best arrangement, I think.

Alice was a slim girl, slim and marvelously attractive, a dark-haired teacher from Seattle off on a free-wheeling trip around the world with her hometown friend Kathy. Happily, Alice and Kathy agreed to join up for a long hike to the base of Mount Everest by way of the high pass at Tesi Lopcha.

We signed on a crew in Kathmandu for a preliminary bus ride to the end of civilization. We signed on a sirdar named Nema, four porters, among them a girl with elaborate rings through her nose, every one able to carry loads of between 80 and 100 pounds in baskets braced to bands around their heads.

But it was slim, vivacious Alice who intrigued me the most.

Pepe Mendez was a part of our party from the very start. Pepe was a big lawyer from Colorado with an enthusiasm for trekking, who had accumulated more than his share of worldly goods. In Kathmandu he checked into a $10 hotel room only because the $30 rooms were full up, while I reluctantly booked a $.60 room in another hotel—I stepped over a woman and two children sleeping in the passageway every morning—because no more $.30 accommodations were available. Despite our obvious differences in the matter of ways and means, Pepe and I shared a mutual taste for adventure.

Outfitted with trekking permits, 400 pounds of food, camping and climbing gear and an itch for the unknown, we started walking in a village called Lamosangu. We walked through thick forests, terraced fields, quiet settlements, deep valleys scooped in the land. Altogether we walked for a total of 30 days.

One morning the track tilted through a forest of maple, the colors ripening into yellows, reds and golds with autumn approaching. Late

Metu, a porter, on the approach march to the base of Mount Everest, Nepal

The author tries on the yeti scalp and finds it fits exactly, at the Pangboche monastery in Nepal.

one afternoon we crossed a covered bridge opening on a rainbow painting the mists over turbulent rapids. In Beding, 12,500 feet up in the Rolwaling Valley, cooking our dinner over a fire of yak dung, a Sherpa woman proudly boasted that she had lived 59 years without ever once taking a bath for fear of antagonizing the evil half-human, half-snake water spirit.

Well above the treeline a day later, traversing an avalanche slope over the edge of a lake, we reached a long, seemingly endless moraine at 16,000 feet. It was very tough going. At sunset we were still far short of the camp, and, while we were traveling at the best pace we could, prospects of arriving before the cold night closed in looked bleak.

Sounds can be deceptive so high in the mountains, whispers echoing into deafening roars, roars muted to whispers, depending. The first time I heard it I couldn't be sure. But the second time some noise bounced off the wall Alice and I interpreted it as a call for help from somewhere behind. With the porters already out of range up ahead, I pelted back down to find Pepe frantically working over Kathy.

Kathy was going numb. Moments later she blacked out entirely, a victim of the thin air feeding far less oxygen. I set out for Nema and the porters, hoping they could carry her to a lower elevation, and fell in an awkward tangle of arms and legs. Stars, rocks, gorges spun round in my head; I almost went blank, too. Even after I got hold of myself and reached the porters, it was too dark to trundle her down.

We put up a makeshift camp right there and spent the night. Kathy was better, markedly better, in the morning, but not up to the rigors ahead. She and Alice took three of the porters and returned to the base, while Pepe and I continued on. Despite the satisfaction of the climb, the fact that Alice had left drilled a hole in my mood. I liked her even more than I had suspected.

We camped on a rock outcrop halfway up the Tesi Lopcha ice fall that night. An astonishing alpenglow painted the mountains a spooky pink, and a plump little pika bounced up my sleeping bag.

At one stage I carried a thirty-pound pac' a vertical sixty-foot ice chimney, ascending prudently, using hea imbing boots, crampons and an ice ax, proud to meet the challenge, proud of my abilities, until I saw our remaining porter come up. Burdened with an eighty-pound pack, he'd covered the same chimney in a pair of tennis shoes.

"These shoes very good," he said when I congratulated him on what seemed a remarkable feat. "They made in China."

We looked into Tibet from Tesi Lopcha, altitude 19,100 feet, picked our way down into the Thami Valley, climbed the high cairn on Kala

Patar, altitude 18,450 feet, where we had a close-up view of what we had come to see.

It lay off to our right, absolutely majestic, a great pile of gray-black rock rising into clear skies, so close it deceptively looked as if its summit might be scaled in a long afternoon, the tallest, most formidable and best-known mountain on God's earth. While there was more for Pepe and me to see, the sight of Mount Everest scaled the next few days to size.

At a ten-cent hotel in Namche Bazar we decided to hike the last eight days by ourselves. We paid off the Sherpas, shipped some gear back and set out without any food or shelter. As we hoped, families along the way were happy to offer meals and lodging for a few rupees, the meals mostly barley meal and rice, potatoes, greens and occasional yak meat, which was quite good, if a bit sinewy.

At one stop we managed to have a prescription breakfast fresh off the roost. Since the trek had given us predictably big appetites, Pepe and I got to arguing how we might equitably divide the three eggs a lady put before us. After listening to our chitchat, she disappeared into a back room. A chicken squawked, and the lady returned with something more than a smile. Now we had four eggs instead of three.

The sleeping arrangements weren't up to Pepe's customary luxury standards. Most of those nights we slept in one big room with a Sherpa family, not to mention any chicken, goats or calves they happened to own. I suppose it balanced out. We wanted to sleep later than the domestic livestock, especially the chickens, allowed, but at least we got off to early starts with roosters performing as advertised a few feet away.

In a ramshackle cottage on one humpbacked mountain I expressed my admiration for a lovely blanket the native woman had woven. Her son expressed a similar interest in my hiking boots. Done. The blanket stuffed in my pack, I walked the last 85 miles of our 30-day, 316-mile hike wearing a pair of sneakers.

Back in Kathmandu I learned that I needed a booster cholera shot for my visa for India. Even under ideal conditions the shot can be painful, of course. In Kathmandu conditions were far from ideal, as young travelers in the area kept telling me. In their opinion it came down to a choice between a new needle or a serious risk of hepatitis from a used model the doctor sunk into one arm after another. I opted for the new needle.

It struck me as a prudent choice when I filed into the only clinic qualified to administer such a shot. The reception area reeked with filth, men, women and children with various afflictions sat against a

The author, Pepe Mendez, and Nema Tenzing pause on Kala Patar (18,450 feet) with Mount Everest rising in the background.

Sherpa sisters in Pangboche, Nepal. They did not know what the author was doing when he took this picture; they just hoped it would not hurt. Their disposition improved after being given a piece of hard candy.

dirty wall, and even the duty nurse looked less antiseptic than I liked. Despite what struck me as a hazardous atmosphere, it took some time to persuade the doctor to use the brand-new needle.

"But my needle very good," he said, underlining the last two words for emphasis. "I use it on many people. No one complain."

Even after he finally agreed, after a slighting reference to fussy Americans, things went badly. He jammed it into my arm without removing the thin, protective wire running through it—perhaps because he'd never handled a new needle before, I glumly suspected. Then the needle exploded in a confetti of glass, steel and serum when he gave it a test squeeze with both hands.

At least the doctor sterilized the community needle now destined for me. In it went, in, in, pumping a syringeful of serum into my system, officially clearing me for passage on to India. But I nervously awaited some sign of a headache, fever or diarrhea for several days.

That encounter with modern medical science at a true grassroots level balanced out in time. I ran into Alice on a crowded street. We warmed immediately to the chance meeting. We walked the city, we had a festive dinner, we made quite a long night of it. Slim and smiling, a venturesome girl with a wonderful sense of curiosity about everything, Alice was exactly the sort of person who could make the world go round for me.

Before our time together ran out I knew that this vagabond school teacher from Seattle was a great prospect for Lloyd Sumner the career bachelor. I knew, but there was nothing to be done. Alice and I were Americans in transit, girdling the globe, forever bound in the wrong directions.

On my last day in Nepal I almost got into real trouble. I almost got into real trouble because my increasingly stereotyped image of Asians was exactly that—a stereotype.

Halfway down a final twist of mountain road running toward the Indian frontier, wheeling through magnificent country on a glassy, sunny day, I came upon a roadblock. I had hit other similar roadblocks before, in other countries, less forbidding than they seemed at first glance, most of them, with the officials generally waving me straight through.

But the roadblock before me that last day in Nepal made me despair. An especially officious guard who might have been assigned a daily quota of abuse—just as some traffic cops back home are assigned a daily quota of speeding tickets—harassed me by asking silly irrelevant questions, demanding papers I had never so much as heard of, treating me with bureaucratic abuse.

My temper finally boiled over. When the pointless interrogation was finished I snatched the passport he so laboriously had been studying and, in my irritation, apparently forgot to zip the pocket of my pack where both the passport and my moneybelt lived. Thus I created the circumstances for what was to be a near disaster.

The steep road I was descending settled into some flatland and I let go at full speed. The bicycle was running beautifully, the wobbly wheel twirling without a hitch, the patches on both tires staying fixed. I passed a heavily settled area, passed people beyond any number walking the road, passed houses, shops, fellow cyclists. I was rolling so fast, in fact, that I literally passed everything on the road, including several trucks piled high with goods.

But one dated old truck, its engine fitfully firing, managed to draw alongside me, then passed by with its horn blasting as it passed. Up ahead the driver came to a stop, gesticulated at me with both arms. Apprehensive, fearing some trouble I couldn't quite identify, I stopped on the opposite side of the road. He called out in a musical burst of Hindi and pointed back up the road.

Quickly I examined the bicycle, the wheels, the pack. The zippered pocket on the pack was wide open; the moneybelt and passport were gone. In my sour view, they were gone for good. After all, I told myself, these people had a dim sense of property rights to start with. Any one of the many Nepalese I had passed along the road need only have picked up what had fallen out of my kit and tucked it away. Finders keepers.

The melancholy course of events was plainly fixed for me. I would have to turn around and try to talk my way past the guard at the roadblock without the crutch of my official documentation. Then I'd have to travel the long road back to Kathmandu to replace the passport and the travelers checks. Worse, what would I live on until I made those arrangements several days away?

As I sat there cursing my fate, a young Nepalese came riding toward me as fast as his old wreck of a bike could carry him. The money belt was swinging on his arm. It hadn't been touched. Passport, travelers checks and some personal papers were all intact, although he could have sold the passport on the flourishing black market and managed to cash the checks, the proceeds of which together would have come to a large fortune by local standards.

He shook his head when I offered a fairly substantial reward.

"No," he said. "No, no. I am just proud I could be of help for you."

Was this the Asia that people had warned me about? Was this the continent rimmed with thieves, pickpockets and worse? Was this the area I myself had sometimes viewed in exactly those terms? Perhaps I had learned a lesson I otherwise would have flunked.

Rolling on toward the Indian frontier, I reflected on some of my dizzying experiences there in Nepal. I thought about my close-up of the tiger, my trek to the base of Mount Everest, my yearning for Alice. And I thought especially about the honesty of the earnest young stranger who had chased me down a long road to return those valuables I couldn't possibly do without.

I couldn't help but wonder whether his kindness reflected the sort of thing that lay ahead in India. Since the next stop was only a blur on the map, another leap into the unknown, I couldn't even guess. But oh how I hoped it was.

Chapter 13

India

According to career travelers who have clocked far more mileage than I have, the bureaucrats assigned to government outposts along the Indian frontier are not widely celebrated for their flexibility. Every so often some especially rigid interpretation of the immigration guidebook—sub clause 11, section F, page 23a, that sort of thing—reportedly does in as much as half a day of an inbound visitor's time, not to mention what remains of his sunny disposition.

In view of all the stories I had heard along the way, I couldn't help but feel a flutter of apprehension when I started across the high ground from Nepal to India. Even the physical layout looked forbidding. Instead of a single office, I was assigned to clear five separate outdoor offices, a sort of bureaucratic mine field, all of them presumably before nightfall, when things might shut down until the next day.

Fortunately, border officials expressed a lively interest in my bicycle, my previous travels, my ultimate goal of spinning clear round the world. The atmosphere became so relaxed that they stamped, sealed, signed and stapled with a splendid efficiency, passing me on to the next office, where I was given the same friendly treatment. In less than an hour I was officially in India.

But as I explained in hopes of soliciting some advice, I was arriving in India without so much as a rupee. The face of the Indian I was talking with folded in a sorrowful expression. Unless I wanted to ride a distance of 60 miles fortified with no coin of the realm, I would have to return to the Nepal side of the border and exchange my money.

In other words, I hadn't beaten the system after all. With my visas for both Nepal and India now officially stamped "USED," there was a chance that I would get caught between the borders, a man without a country where he could spend the night, a shuttlecock marooned by red tape. It looked very much as if the notorious bureaucratic chicken feathers had got me.

But a few more words with the five offices, a few smiles, a few answers to questions about my bicycle tour and I crossed from one land back to another, a wad of rupees in my pocket. It wasn't a moment too soon, either. Perhaps twenty miles of sun still stood in the sky for me to wheel the thirty miles on to the nearest spot to sleep for the night.

As things turned out, it was hardly worth the strain of my boisterous ride. In Pharanda, a dry scruffy village crowded with livestock as well as people, I slept on bare springs with no mattress in an unlit room in the government inspection house, only not for long.

At dawn I went spinning south, then west, egrets, parrots and cranes providing a splash of color along the roadway. Men bundled in blankets on bullock carts shared the road too, clopping slowly from here to there, another trip in a long routine. Some of them, who must have traveled all night, were actually asleep and trusted the bullock to follow the cart ahead. There were times when I wished I could switch on a similar kind of auto-pilot myself.

Beyond the narrow winding streets of Gorakhpur, where a sikh in a splashy purple turban and a braided beard treated me to a cup of tea, the countryside turned bright green. Animals were fat, crops looked healthy, nobody begged for food. Briefly, very briefly, the old tintype of India as a suffering land of ignorance, poverty and inefficiency looked a slander to me.

In Basti, madcap, picturesque Basti, with the restaurants easy to locate because they attracted the largest swarm of flies, hand prints showing in the cow dung plastered against the side of houses to dry, I found that the abiding image was all too accurate. This was especially so in the matter of astonishing inefficiency, on which India generally may hold the copyright.

Before I officially could sign on at a bungalow where I was assigned to spend the night, for instance, I had to embark on a loony paper chase from one end of Basti to another. I called on a caretaker, an executive engineer, a civic official, another official of loftier rank and then the engineer again, almost three hours spinning my wheels before a room in the bungalow was mine. The process might have gone faster if only they posted names on the streets I had to find.

Later I ordered a pair of pants, which, at local prices, even I could

Typical traffic throughout India

afford. During a babble of jovial small talk, the tailor said yes, positively, absolutely, no doubt about it, the pants would be ready by eight o'clock, not an instant later. I could count on him, he told me, he was an honorable man who never breached his word. Maybe not. But the pants were not ready when I returned for them.

"You must realize this is India." The tailor, a cockeyed little man with a bad leg, seemed perplexed that I actually expected them. "If I say for sure at eight, I mean maybe at nine. It is the custom."

The trousers were finished after a further delay, and I slipped into them and cycled west again. I passed through Ayodhya, Faizabad and Lucknow, crowded cities, noisy and boiling, filled with tired old men, bedraggled women, children running ragged through the dirty streets. Ayodhya struck me as a real anomaly. By actual count it has 6,500 Hindu temples but not a single restaurant, which is good for the soul, if not the digestive system. Vendors did peddle a restricted assortment of vegetarian foods but no meats, not even eggs.

Soft drinks with only a mild flavor were still harder to come by in the ancient city where Prince Rama had been born. The far-off taste of ginger ale, root beer, cola drinks spun in my memory. But after a futile search I made do with a small bottle of sweet cough syrup.

In Lucknow the bill-of-fare was more substantial. I treated myself to an extravagant dinner: asparagus soup and chicken cutlets, espresso coffee and two dishes of pistachio ice cream. After all, it was Christmas day, my fourth Christmas on the high road leading around the world, and I felt entitled to some extravagance.

In an old Marx Brothers film Groucho, enacting the role of Captain Spalding the famous African explorer with his usual irreverence, stared straight at the camera and went into a tangled monologue. "I just shot an elephant in my pajamas," he said, rolling his eyes. "What he was doing in my pajamas I'll never know."

I have never shot an elephant in my pajamas, God forbid, but I expect Groucho never saw twenty black monkeys sitting on a white picket fence. I did. I saw them a few miles outside of Lucknow as I pedaled west for Kanpur and the Ganges.

The sight of the monkeys—twenty, count them, twenty—haunted

Ayodhya, India, where the author experienced a very atypical Christmas Eve

Monkeys on the street, Faizabad, India

me long after the fence faded behind me. Did they amount to some kind of symbol? If so, was it favorable or otherwise, plus or minus, a good omen or a curse?

A curse, a jolting series of adverse events told me soon enough. In the middle of a bridge I pulled out to pass a motorcycle, heard a bicycle bell behind me, saw the motorcycle swerve and drive me into a car coming the other way. Surprisingly, everyone escaped unharmed except for my bike, which suffered a bent rim I straightened as best I could.

Later that day an approaching bull cart almost filled the narrow road I was riding. Just as we were slowly squeezing past each other a teen-age Indian boy, anxious to talk with me, rushed out in front of the bike. My options were alarmingly limited. Either I hit the boy or hit the bull, simple as that. I chose the bull, grabbed a sharp, brightly painted horn to avoid being gored. An assessment after the handlebars and horns were untangled revealed no serious injuries—and a growing suspicion that those twenty black monkeys were more than they seemed.

Later, still later, I had a head-on collision with a water buffalo, although it damaged mostly my ego. The curious events unfolding one after another spooked me to a point where I was riding badly. Before dusk a wild parrot, who wasn't navigating very well, either, banged into my kneecap, painful, the most painful experience of the day.

At a restaurant in Agra several days later a fortune teller at least had the candor to admit he was putting a curse on me after trying to bamboozle some small change. A tall gaunt man wearing a tattered sheet, he fixed me with a rheumy eye, went into what must have been a standard spiel, subject to change.

"You are from America," he said, with the colors showing on my bicycle. "You are on a long journey. You are worried about your girl friend. You are going to pay me for telling you this."

"You didn't get the last part of that right, neighbor," I said. "Why should I pay you for things I already know?"

Put to a challenge, he dipped deeper into his bag of prophecies. "You will not be married in the near future." He affected a mock good cheer. "You will die in your own home at age seventy-one. You will receive a telegram in two weeks saying you will receive a large sum of money." His vision of imminent riches was plainly calculated to set me up for what was to follow. "Now you will pay me fifty rupees." On the basis of his sliding scale I must have looked good for precisely that sum.

But since I had in no way solicited his forecast, I filed a strenuous objection.

"No, I won't," I said. "I didn't ask for the information. I won't pay for it."

"Then I have no choice." The old boy shrugged his bony shoulders. "Then I must put a curse on you."

As things turned out, he was more effective in the curse department than he was unwrapping the future. That big money telegram didn't arrive, still hasn't, in fact, although I keep hoping. But my situation otherwise deteriorated almost immediately. I left Agra running at both ends, with a head cold and another drumming case of diarrhea. A strong wind rose against me, the boiling sun beating down on the road caused my lip to fester and crack open again.

But the truck drivers booming along the road were the worst of it. They had an angry contempt for everyone, cyclists especially, and deliberately crowded them off the track, even if it meant crossing the center line in pursuit of these targets. They were primitives, most of them, primitives with too much horsepower to burn, the reincarnation of Shiva, the Hindu god of destruction.

I did the best I could in my own competition with these bullyboys.
If a truck came straight at me, I lowered my flagstaff to a 45 degree
angle and scratched the cab of the truck. This caused several to give
way, but drove some others to a greater fury. One of them grabbed
at the staff, clawed the flag off as he went by.

On a whim I decided that I might just as well see whether I happened to possess any powers of darkness myself. Any time a truck tried
to force me over I laid a Virginia-accented, made-in-America
whammy on it in hopes of proper vengeance. Before the day lapsed
I came upon not one but six disabled trucks—overturned, smashed
into a tree, down for the count with engine trouble, two tires flat, a
load missing, the last of them surrounded by a violent crowd angrily
surrounding the driver—that I recognized as specific victims of my
curse, which was either a great coincidence or suggested I'd been in
the wrong line of work for a long time.

Fellow cyclists could be a problem too, not because they had the
same brute instincts, but because many of them had a free-wheeling
approach to safety. Sometimes I ran my own bike up to 25 miles an
hour for several miles in an attempt to stretch some distance ahead
of especially hazardous brothers of the spoke, which drained my vitality in the smothering Indian heat.

If the days were often a burden crossing the swollen belly of India,
however, the nights were a delight. Whenever I could manage it I
stayed in DAK rest houses, clean, spacious, inexpensive bungalows
built for touring government officials and otherwise available to
foreign tourists.

In Shivpuri, the bungalow sat in a national park, the building a
former sailing lodge for British officers before the sun set on the Em-
pire, which ought to suggest its splendid comforts. I sat in a spacious
private courtyard—my four-room suite cost $.65—focusing on ante-
lope and spotted deer, peafowl and several varieties of pheasant. At
dusk I reflected on the great distance I had covered and spun an occasional dream of my eventual return home to Virginia.

In India the weeks seemed a jumble, confused and disjoined, a time
warp in a huge sprawling land. For the sake of a more rigid schedule
I assigned myself a fixed distance of seventy miles every day, not a
mite more even when I felt up to pushing on. But generally, seventy
miles was sufficient.

Despite its position on the map, India is crisp in the morning, raw
and cold. I dressed in woolen climbing knickers, sweaters and mittens.
Soon I learned to stop for a warming cup of tea any time I saw a group
of men huddled round a roadside fire. With the sun starting to burn a

hole in the sky in midmorning, I peeled down to a T-shirt and a pair of shorts, trimmed my speed, stretched for seventy quota miles.

Moments, flavorful moments, rise out of the jumble of the long ride from Agra to Bombay. Women tightly wrapped in colorful saris carried baskets of fruit on their heads. Eight, nine, as many as a dozen crowded into three-wheeled taxis legally built for only four passengers. At one point I saw a dog feeding on the carcass of a dead cow while a wedge of buzzards patiently waited their turn. Inexplicably, an experience I can't interpret even now, I rode past several genuine Indian Indians living in tepees. It was as astonishing as those twenty black monkeys on the white picket fence.

The first time I saw the Taj Mahal it shimmered in the pale blue light of a full moon, fluted and perfect, a wonder of the world so spectacular that it caught at the throat. The delicate inlaid marble work, the symmetrical gates beyond, the clean sweeping lines showing in the moonlight had an almost hypnotic effect, although I still preferred the spectacular mosque back in Kuala Kangsar.

The second time I saw the Taj Mahal I nearly didn't see it at all, for reasons that have as much to do with official Indian security as they do with me. Returning to the edifice first thing the following morning to shoot some pictures by daylight, I was suspiciously eyed by several guards. When I reached the main gate that suspicion bulged into an official No Trespass.

The bristling security was due to a state visit by the president of the United Arab Emirates, who was scheduled a few hours later. I did the best I could. In emphatic tones I told the head guard at the main gate that a round-the-world cyclist was as important as the head of some two-bit country. But we both of us actually knew better. I wasn't sitting on a great gusher of oil.

Since the guards had seen me prowling the approaches to the Taj Mahal earlier, they nourished a feeling that I was a firebrand intending to plant a bomb. The more I argued, the more convinced they became. In the end they ordered me—in stiff, no-nonsense English— to get out of the area until the afternoon. I got.

On my return for a set of pictures later I passed through a key gate just as the visiting president himself came the other way. Visibly alarmed to see me so close, several guards warned me to stop unless I wanted to be shot. I stopped. But I permitted myself the childish pleasure of making monkey faces at the Middle Eastern oilbag as he was driven by.

My occasional conflicts riding across India were in no way restricted
to officious security people assigned to chaperone off-shore VIP's. I
had my problems with cafe owners, lodge keepers, taxi drivers, truck-
ers, travel agents and everyday Indian civilians. I experienced great
pleasures, more than I can properly count, but a few of the prickly
moments still linger in my mind.

In Agra a number of rickshaw drivers competed for the privilege
of driving me to the hotel, where I would collect my bike. In the end
I chose to do business with the one who offered me an eight-mile ride
for one rupee, or $.12 U.S., which was so cheap I really ought to have
known better. Brimming with good cheer, he started to hustle me before we reached the first corner.

"Your hotel is no good," he said, showing a mouthful of decaying
teeth. "I take you to a better hotel."

"No," I said. "I've left my things there. The Starlight Hotel, please,
fast as you can."

"Shall we go to the Taj first?"

"No. I've seen it already. The Starlight Hotel, please."

"I have a friend who makes ivory table." I had to give him credit
for impressive resolve. "We'll go there, yes."

"No."

"After the hotel I can take you somewhere else."

"No. I have a bicycle at the hotel." On hearing this he spun round.
"Why are we going back?"

"I'm going back to the station," he said.

"You are not going back to the station. You are taking me directly
to my hotel, the Starlight Hotel, with no stops on the way, or else I
will have to report you to the authorities. I've already written down
your number."

Obediently he turned. Obediently he pedaled me slowly toward
the hotel, until he found another rickshaw driver willing to take me
the rest of the way. Obviously I was a poor mark for a free-enterpriser
who depended more on assorted kickbacks than basic wages running
a rickshaw.

The head man of a small village where I paused en route for Bombay thoughtfully supplied me with a hell-fire brand of chili and some
ginger tea. When I asked for water, I was given a glass of colored liquid
crawling with wildlife. I asked if it had been boiled.

"Not necessary," he said. "We drink this water all the time."

"Would you please boil it for me, please?"

"Water all right. I drink some myself. See."

An edge of resentment began to ripple through the crowd of natives when I resisted. What to do? I didn't want to offend anyone, not after their show of generosity. Reluctantly, very reluctantly, I drank the water.

If my bowels didn't constrict immediately, it didn't take long. I swallowed an Enterovioform tablet to fight the diarrhea, offered up my thanks for the thick protective countryside I was traveling, although there was really no need for modesty. While sufficient trees were available, many locals relieved themselves wherever they felt the need, such as in front of shops on city streets.

Officially, at least, the government took a dim view of that informal exposure. In one city, I forget exactly which one, a billboard tried to fix some social graces: "When Nature Calls Have An Answer, But Do You Have To Have An Audience?"

Once I finally approached Bombay the whole speckled tour of India dramatically improved in ways I could appreciate. Bananas, chocolates and meat, the bonanza I left far behind, were available again. Trucks stayed on their own side of the road and cyclists kept their distance. A cooling wind shifted, making the days less onerous, helping the painful split on my lip heal.

In Bombay I happily accepted an invitation to stay with relatives of some friends from the University of Virginia, whose generous hospitality restored my energy. Among countless other kindnesses, they arranged long tours in and around Bombay, served a number of memorable Indian meals and explained the Zoroastrian religion they practiced, which, while I hadn't so much as heard of it before, I found fascinating, especially their manner of disposing of the dead.

Since Zoroastrians take a flinty view of polluting the environment, they cannot bury the dead for fear of polluting the soil or cremate them for fear of polluting the atmosphere. What they do instead is to leave bodies in enormous Towers of Silence, where they are picked clean by buzzards, which pollutes nothing at all, except for the birds, I suppose. I walked past the towers once for a look at the buzzards, big and understandably fat, wheeling in the clear sky awaiting their next meal.

Enjoyable as my stopover was, it seemed time to get on with the tour. I saw a doctor for a yellow fever shot, had my handlebar bag repaired, bought a ticket on the *Harsha Vardhana*. Just across the Arabian Sea lay the wonders of Africa, not the least of them Kilimanjaro and Victoria Falls, both of them very much on my flexible itinerary. I had come a long way, but I still had a distance to go, no matter how I performed, which reminded me of a dialogue the old

Army football flash Glen Davis experienced during his brief post-graduate fling as a professional.

After Davis ran a kickoff ninety-five yards for a spectacular touch-down in a practice game in training camp, a fastidious assistant coach with the Los Angeles Rams pulled him aside for a peckish critique. To hear him tell it, Davis failed to follow his interference properly, forgot to switch the ball from one arm to another after reversing his field, and hadn't used a stutter-step when he should have.

"Well, coach, how was it for distance?" Davis plaintively inquired.

I could put much the same question. For all the emotional ups and downs, all the frustrations, all the jousts with belligerent truck drivers and all the stooptag diarrhea along the way, I had wheeled more than 1,300 miles across India. How was *that* for distance, coach?

Chapter 14

Africa East

The *Harsha Vardhana* was only one-third full, which meant nobody objected when I rode around one of the decks every day to stay in shape. This deck cycling was especially thrilling when the ship rolled to the ocean's swells. By carefully timing my turns at each side, I never stopped coasting. It was a cyclist's dream, downhill, downhill forever.

One day I'd coasted almost an hour when I misjudged the ship's roll, crashed into a post. A sharp pain pierced my right side, and I feared I had broken some ribs. This persistent pain plus learning that I wouldn't be allowed to cycle in the game parks, and reports of cholera in Tanzania, knee-deep mud on the roads in Malawi, an ominous political situation in Mozambique, and oppressive heat everywhere on my route prompted me to give up a little of my independence.

Dave Tinney, a slight dark-haired Englishman also on the *Harsha Vardhana*, who had brought his Landrover along, planned to drive leisurely to Johannesburg on roughly the same route I hoped to cycle. He was easily persuaded to travel at roughly my pace, climb Mount Kilimanjaro with me, sometimes carry my luggage, give me a lift through the game parks, and often camp with me for safety. In return I would pay a share of his petrol.

At Mombasa in Kenya, I was almost refused entry because I had only $430 for a planned stay of one month. The official wouldn't believe I could live on $2 a day, although I had lived on less, under $1,

Bicycling across the ocean. Between India and Africa, the author enjoyed riding around the deck of the Harsha Vardhana, *especially when he could ride the ocean's rolls and coast continuously.*

in fact, elsewhere. He stamped my passport only after I produced a year-old letter from my bank describing my emergency money. He even waived the deposit usually required on bicycles.

Mombasa's streets were wide, clean, exciting, walked by more whites than blacks. Shops were well stocked, restaurants served Western food. Could this be the Africa of song and legend? My first stop was for a box of Kentucky Fried Chicken, of all things. Colonel Sanders, remember me? I cycled into the countryside without pausing to prime my mind for another culture. People were courteous and intelligent. Drivers actually stopped for crosswalks and left ample room when they passed. Only my sensitive rib cage prevented an enjoyable ride to the campground at Kanamai, ten miles to the north.

As I approached the campground I got to feeling guilty about that fried chicken. All seven Europeans off the ship and I had boasted to each other how we always ate local food for the sake of widening our interests.

"Hi, Lloyd," Dave shouted. "You made it here really fast. Have you eaten?

"Yeah. I got a bite in town."

"Where did you eat?"

"Oh, a little restaurant. How about you?"

"I found a little restaurant, too."

"African food?"

"Not exactly, but it was good."

Eventually I discovered that every blinking one of us had stopped at the same fried chicken place, guiltily thinking everyone else was eating local dishes.

Next morning I cycled to a free hospital, where a pretty young nurse whisked me to the front of the line. The Indian woman doctor performed a simple test and said that my ribs were bruised, not broken, although I was given a prescription for codeine to ease the pain.

I settled in for a week of leisurely camping in a coconut grove while my ribs healed. The days fluttered by, gentle breezes, swaying palms, cooling swims in the ocean, runs down the beach, skin diving over coral. It was hard to leave for the dry sweltering interior.

But the urge to see big game finally drove me to hop on the bike one morning and ride hard toward Nairobi. I cycled through the lush coastal zone of sisal plantations and giant baobabs, trees with thick, gnarled trunks and small, spindling branches, into the desolate savannah. My saddlebags in Dave's keeping, I pedaled easily up a road forever uphill in equatorial sun every bit as vicious as it had been in Thailand. Near the entrance to Tsavo West National Park, I crouched in the sparse shade of a thorn bush to wait for Dave. The moment he arrived, we were robbed, sort of, anyway.

Dave had just opened the back door when his leg was ferociously attacked. He screamed, leaped away. A big baboon jumped in, grabbed two loaves of bread, and disappeared in a furry flash. There followed a frisky game of cops and robbers involving two men and twenty baboons. The robbers got away with the bread, the cops got only a few pictures.

Inside the gate, the animals were friendlier and less aggressive. An old elephant, a giraffe whose neck stretched up, up, up, and several cape buffalo shared a waterhole when we stopped to watch. Later more than 100 elephants ambled across the road. A tiny dik-dik, only slightly larger than the mouse deer of Malaysia, strolled precariously in their midst.

In the next few days we saw large numbers of big game animals, not the least of them an enormous black-maned lion enjoying the

shade, snuffling near the road. Despite my passion for wild animals, I
was rather disappointed. After three and a half years on a bicycle,
it was hard to appreciate animals—or anything else—from the window of a car. If only I could cycle those lonely roads all by myself.

The nights were intriguing. Most of the nocturnal chorus was sooth-
ing and harmonious, but the occasional shriek of a baboon, rising like
a siren, could awaken even me. We saw tracks of lions within a mile
of camp, but our closest call came when a large elephant tromped
through only fifteen feet from where I slept.

At Mzima Springs, Dave and I decided to stalk four elephants
marching single file in front of us. Suddenly in perfect unison they
all turned, flapping their ears, trumpeting, moving fast. I froze. They
charged to within a few yards, turned away. I have an elephant's
memory about that vivid incident.

As we traveled around the park, I looked more at Kilimanjaro—
floating high in the humid air, abiding, a majestic vision—than at
the animals. I wanted to cycle straight to the mountain but we had
to get visas in Nairobi. No tickee, no Kilimanjaro.

While the visas were being processed, Dave and I toured the Mount
Kenya area and Lake Nakaru, famous for its millions of flamingos.
When we saw only half a dozen of the tall, pink birds I asked a native
where the rest were. He said, "Nakaru have many birds. Tourists come
see birds. City built for tourists stay. City waste make lake water bad.
Birds go away."

On returning to Nairobi I bought two new tires, started cycling
due south while Dave stayed behind to find some additional riders to
share expenses. It was a fine ride. The dawn air was cool, the road
was smooth, the traffic was light. The snowy summit of Kilimanjaro
loomed in the distance, teasing me with a brief view through the trees,
drawing me like a magnet. Hundreds of gazelles, impalas, ostriches,
and giraffes watched as I cycled through their grazing grounds. This
was the ideal seat to see the game. Masai tribesmen, with their elaborate headgear, fancy beadwork, and earlobes dangling almost on their
shoulders, curiously watched and waved at my passing.

Once while I fixed a flat tire, the shadow of a tall man fell on me.
Looming over me was a red-robed, elderly Masai herdsman, ears
plugged with inch-wide dowels of wood, hair tightly braided, neck
ringed with colorful beads, his hand holding a long staff. He stood
only a foot away. After two minutes of mutual staring, he mumbled
something in singsong Swahili that I took to be an offer of help. I shook
my head and made rolling motions with my hands to show that every-

thing was all right. He stood in the shade of a nearby tree and watched until I rode away.

When I stopped for lunch a boy similarly appeared from nowhere. His legs bore long white scratches, looking like a map of random country roads. He was a cattle herder too, but more animated. He walked in big circles around Maria, and thanked me for a share of my bread and beans, with a broad smile.

Late that day I crossed the Tanzania border into a communist society where white "imperialists" like me are unpopular. Nobody smiled, spoke, or waved. Nobody would tell me where I could sleep. The people walked in the road, pressed close when I stopped, and threw clods of dirt at me when I tried to take a picture. Pictures without a modeling fee took their soul away, as one man explained.

After camping in a secluded grove of trees, I rolled into Arusha, where several young men offered phenomenally favorable rates of exchange on money. Fortunately, I had been tipped off. Africans get more money from reporting tourists who change illegally than they get on the exchange. Only the Asians, fearful of being ejected from the country at any time, could be trusted for unofficial exchanges. I changed a little money at a bank and pedaled directly east toward Moshi on the southern slopes of Kilimanjaro.

There I went to the stunning, modern, ranch-style house of Carlos and Myrtice Owens, Southern Baptist missionaries to Tanzania for twenty years. A couple of servants worked in the vast garden; the life of a missionary was not as rough as I had imagined. After seeing that I had neither long hair nor a beard, they invited me to spend the night. It was almost like being home again. Southern accents, southern food, religious talk.

Reverend Owens explained some of my observations of Tanzania. "Part of the government's plan to encourage people to move to communes is to burn their private houses," he said. "This, along with the shortages of many kinds of goods, causes the people to be less friendly than in Kenya."

"How well is communism working here?"

"Not very well. With all due respect, I'm afraid the African is just not the sort to hoe his neighbor's garden."

"In most communist countries, religion is discouraged. How have you been allowed to stay?"

"So far the government has not interfered with the church except to the point of sometimes holding political meetings on Sunday morning and having mandatory attendance. Some people believe that

Christian teaching runs counter to Marxism, but I stay completely out of politics. I stay busy just doing the Lord's work. Are you a Christian?"

"I was raised in a Christian home, attended church every Sunday for sixteen years, and have read the Bible several times, but I am still seeking."

"Surely in all your travels you have realized the truth of the Bible and the inadequacies of paganism."

"On the contrary. I saw a Hindu woman's prayer answered with indisputable certainty. I saw an uneducated folk doctor cure me in five minutes of my only attack of severe illness. I saw Buddhists living lives certain to be pleasing to any god."

"But if they don't know Jesus, they are lost. Do you still go to church?"

"Not much. I've been in churches from small wooden buildings of the Appalachians to the great cathedrals of Europe, but I never felt even remotely as close to God in any of them as I feel when I climb a mountain, walk through wilderness or cycle through jungle or desert."

I quoted a verse from the good book before riding away, "'I will lift mine eyes unto the hills from whence cometh my help,'" which was perfectly true.

I rode the twenty-five uphill miles to Marangu, the starting point of the climb, caught up with Dave and his new riders—Ray, a round-faced, red-headed Englishman who had been robbed in Nairobi, Brenda and Barb, two vagabond girls from Canada, Judith from New Zealand. Judith, being slightly overweight and having little interest in mountains, volunteered to stay behind and guard the bike and the Landrover while the rest of us climbed the mountain.

The hardest, most forbidding part about climbing Kilimanjaro is to get started. The Tanzanian government requires all parties to stay in their huts and hire a guide and a porter for the guide. The cost ranges from $7.00 if you carry your own equipment, do your own cooking, and change money with the Asians to $150.00 if the hotel arranges everything, porters carry your pack and do your cooking. I chose the lesser amount. I carry my own pack as a matter of principle. The others hired porters in the hope that they would increase their chance of success.

The guide served us well: we saw him a total of two hours during the entire five-day trip. The porters were fine except for occasional petty thefts. Chocolate was not available in Tanzania, and they could not resist our supply.

Starting from 5,000 feet, we climbed slowly through farmland, banana and coffee plantations and forests to reach the first hut at 9,000 feet. From there a verdant rain forest, complete with Spanish moss, opened to the moorland with great views of Kibo and Mwenzi, the two peaks of Kilimanjaro. I asked a couple on their way down if they had made the summit. "Of course. We're Swiss."

On the third day we arrived at Kibo Hut, elevation 15,000 feet, and went to bed at two in the afternoon with heavy snow falling outside. Brenda and Barb, without adequate sleeping bags, tried sleeping together for warmth. Still cold, they sought the warmer ones in the hut. Brenda chose Dave, Barb chose Ray. I felt somewhat slighted, miffed, really, but at least I got more sleep than they did.

As planned, we arose at 12:30 A.M., had some hot tea and porridge, pulled on all of our clothes. I didn't have a down parka, so I wrapped my sleeping bag around my body under a wind parka. Then we stepped out into the bitter cold air by the light of a full moon with three or four inches of snow underfoot.

I slipped off ahead, zigzagging on the snow-covered scree, answering the summit's call, not knowing exactly what lay ahead beyond the mountain and the moon. Dark shadows appeared on the sides, faded away below. The top of the scree appeared no nearer, but it didn't really matter.

For two and a half hours I climbed alone. I lost the track, climbed some difficult rock and watched the moon go behind Kibo, which left me in darkness. One big boulder, another, still another. A pullup, a layback, a short scramble and I was on the rim. Now the light was just emerging behind Mwenzi. Across the crater the full moon prepared to set as the sun got ready to rise. I climbed on to Gilman's Point. Below I heard a scramble and saw a silhouette—Feras the guide, who seemed disgusted he had to climb so far to catch me.

"You wait for sun, then go down, yes?" Feras suggested hopefully.

"No, I wait for sun, then go to Uhuru. You may go down. I am good climber. I climb alone."

Uhuru, the true summit, was another hour and a half away. Only one climber in ten bothers to go beyond this low point on the crater rim. At the moment the sun was supposed to show, I stole away and climbed a nearby peak for an uninterrupted view of the sun rising up over a horizon 240 miles away. The jagged silhouette of Mwenzi was just below.

To the north the elaborate hanging glaciers of the icefield sprung to life as the endless terraces received the sun, reflected a different shade of alpenglow pink. Inside the crater ice towers, looking like

Ice towers near the summit of Mount Kilimanjaro, Tanzania

calcite stalagmites in a well-adorned southern cave, formed still another unearthly fairyland.

I drifted on through eight-inch snow and across a few glaciers toward the highest point in Africa. Every step brought a new and inspiring scene—200-foot-high glacier faces, carved ice towers, distant mountains, faraway plains.

I reveled on top for half an hour before Ray arrived. The rest had turned back earlier. On the descent we picked up Dave at Kibo Hut, and the three of us dropped to Horombo Hut and shared it with five airline stewardesses from Minnesota. They had paid $175 each for the climb, were not having a good time, were shocked that they had to share the hut with men. Some fun, that evening.

At Marangu we caught up with Brenda and Barb, who could not get off the mountain fast enough. They descended the whole thirty miles in one day. Brenda had wrap-around blisters on her toes that wouldn't heal for a month. Ray and I also met the Swiss couple. They asked how we had fared and I could not resist, "Of course we reached the summit. We're *not* Swiss."

In great spirits I rolled down the long hill from Marangu, aiming for some place beyond the far southern horizon, at last seriously on my way toward Capetown, 2,500 air miles away. The countryside was surprisingly green and sparsely populated. The bike rode as smoothly as she ever had despite her nearly 24,000 miles.

The author on the summit of Mount Kilimanjaro

All went well until just south of Tanga, where some officers ordered me to stop. An outbreak of cholera in the area had killed several people. Travelers were allowed only to pass through the area quickly without stopping. I crawled into the shade of some sharp-spiked sisal plants and waited for Dave to come along and give me a lift over the dangerous area.

When we passed that stretch, I started cycling again. I followed a pattern of riding hard in the coolness of the morning, resting often in the hot afternoon, and usually camping with Dave and his crew. We camped in open fields, beside police stations, on golf courses, where addicts are allowed a second ball with no penalty stroke if crocodiles come too close. Since my companions slept late, lingered over breakfast, and lazily broke camp, our progress across Africa was about the same. In many ways this arrangement was the best of both worlds. I mingled with the people enough to satisfy my curiosity but did not have to tolerate them to the point of frustration. I had plenty of time alone but also friends to camp with.

While I was cycling, people were outwardly friendly, but when I

Pastoral scene in Tanzania. Although this lioness looks very cuddly, stomach rubbing is not recommended.

stopped to talk, the conversation often turned sour. One nicely dressed young man talked with intelligence and enthusiasm, then suddenly said, "You must provide me with money because I haven't any in my pocket."

An older gentleman held my arm and welcomed me to his village. He even ordered the storekeeper to sell me a Fanta that he was keeping out of sight. As I was enjoying this refreshment and friendship, the old man frowned, gripped my arm harder, and demanded to see my "permit." Not knowing what he meant and having left my passport in the Landrover, I made up a cock-and-bull story, filled it with big words and important names, bowed respectfully, pulled away and pedaled hard down the road.

Cycling became more enjoyable in southern Tanzania. In the cool mornings I often rode twenty miles an hour. People became friendlier. A taxi driver stopped near the Zambia border to offer me a free ride. I accepted, holding onto his door handle for a few miles as he warned me about the severe restrictions of the Malawi customs. I passed easily through the unpopulated, extreme northeast corner of Zambia, waited for Dave before approaching the Malawi border, hoping for safety in numbers.

When they arrived, Dave and I cut our hair, Ray took a tuck in his bell-bottomed trousers, the girls put on long dresses. A woman can be immediately detained without bail and fined $250 in Malawi for wearing a miniskirt or shorts in public. The penalty for bell-bottomed trousers is even greater.

Still, the officials in Chitipa spent three hours searching everything we had and querying us about our experience in Tanzania. We innocently endangered our entry by relating only favorable stories. As we learned later, Malawi had better relations with South Africa than with Tanzania.

Dave drove on ahead while I cycled the dusty, rocky road toward the northern end of Lake Malawi. By midafternoon, the combination of sun and dust was wearing me down when I saw Dave's Landrover on a slight incline. He was not camping. He was out of petrol. And in the circumstances he was delighted to see me.

I cycled on to Karonga for petrol with no Malawi money, the banks closed and shops reluctant to handle foreign currency. I stopped first at the Oilcom station, was sent to the Shell station, then to the post office, then to the district commissioner, who was not in, a frustrating game of musical chairs. I tried to exchange money in shops but every merchant refused. Finally an Asian salesman gave me a Kwacha for a dollar—a good rate of exchange—which bought one gallon of petrol.

The many days of racing a Landrover caught up with me next morning. The sun rose before I did, and the day was already sticky hot. I decided to join Dave on a side trip up the Livingstonia Escarpment. Halfway up the Landrover ran out of petrol again, and again my faithful bicycle was called to the rescue. I began to cycle up the steep rocky road toward Livingstonia. I enjoyed the two-hour climb along the six-foot-wide rocky track. In some ways, it reminded me of the jungle mountains of Sumatra, but the urgency of the mission destroyed the tranquility. On the crest of the ridge, the rocks gave way to a dirt surface and Livingstonia was not in sight. The road dropped to a small village then climbed again. Rain, the first I had seen since Thailand, began to turn the dirt into sticky, gooey mud, which stuck to the tires and bogged me down. The tricks learned on the jungle track in Malaysia did not work here. The mud was like clay and resisted being pulled loose. I tried pushing, but the bike just would not go. I trudged on, Maria on my shoulder, until my shoes finally fell apart. I then hid the bike beneath some leafy bushes and walked barefoot the last two miles to Livingstonia. I was mud-caked, weak with hunger and soaked by the heavy rain.

At Livingstonia, I found the petrol pump was closed. No one knew when the owner might arrive but the next pump, someone said, was only forty-seven miles farther on. I sat down on a picnic table, blew the raindrops off my nose, and wondered what to do. It had taken four and a half hours to get this far. I searched around the mission for half an hour and found some cookies and a soft drink for sale. Finally, the petrol man showed up and sold me a gallon. As I slogged back, Ray, tired of listening to the girls arguing with Dave, came to meet me.

When we got back to Maria, the rain had stopped, and Ray insisted on cycling. On his first turn the back wheel went flat and he either didn't know or didn't care but kept right on riding, which totally ruined the tube. We had to half-roll, half-carry Maria all the way back down. We arrived at the car in time to see a local truck emptying petrol into it. I decided then I would stick to cycling. It was easier, less frustrating, and much faster.

Every time I stopped en route to Blantyre and the Mozambique border I was warned against cycling across that country. One man had been seriously injured when a land mine blew up his jeep. A hitchhiking girl had been raped and taken prisoner by the Frelimo. A motorcyclist had been robbed at one road block and stopped again two miles down the road. According to locals, the various liberation groups manning the road blocks were satisfied with food and cigarettes. But, knowing how often natives had coveted my bicycle, I feared I might not get by so easily.

In Blantyre Dave, his gang, and I stayed at the home of Ted Rankin, a white Rhodesian whom we had met in Lilongwe. I went to the American embassy for extra pages in my passport, visited the American library for one last memory of home, and bought the first pack of cigarettes in my life.

At the urging of the American consul I accepted Dave's offer of a lift across the wild neck of Mozambique.

I rode to the frontier, and when Dave arrived I strapped the bike on top of his Landrover. We rolled on to the border. A nervous Portuguese official demanded an $8 visa fee from each of us before stamping our passports. Then three Frelimo guards, automatic rifles slung over their shoulders, started a thorough search.* We let them go through a couple of bags, then casually offered them cigarettes and fresh, buttered rolls. They relaxed, smiled and waved us through, a savings of at least an hour. The time was precious as the Rhodesian border closed at six, and we didn't want to be marooned in Mozambique overnight.

At each of the other three road blocks, we handed out more cigarettes and fresh, buttered rolls. The heavily armed guards, many in their teens, responded with only a token search. So crossing Mozambique was comfortably anticlimactic.

Yet one last hurdle none of us had foreseen still remained. Greatly relieved to have survived Mozambique, we walked into the building housing Rhodesian customs. A sign greeted us with bad news: "Entry granted only to persons holding an air ticket to leave Rhodesia and at least $350." Brenda and Barb had tickets but not one of us had the money. Luck, however, was on our side. The officer in charge had just been fired and in his agitation never even asked to see our resources.

My spirits were doubly high as I cycled the lightly traveled road from Bulawayo to Victoria Falls. The countryside was often wild and lovely but my eyes rarely left my odometer for long. The numbers were clicking around to a major milestone. According to the *Rand McNally World Atlas*, the distance around the earth at the equator is 24,901 miles. Just before ten o'clock on Easter Sunday, 1975, at an overlook

---

*Lest the reader think it odd that the Portuguese official was hobnobbing with the guerrillas who fought against Portuguese rule, this incident took place in the transition period before Mozambique became independent.

Maria views the mist-filled gorge of Victoria Falls, Rhodesia, as her odometer registers 24,901 miles, the exact distance around the world.

of Victoria Falls, my odometer turned over 24,901 miles since leaving Ridgeway—my first "world."

Dave and his crowd met me at the Victoria Falls Hotel with a big sign of congratulations, a bottle of champagne, a huge lighted candle, and a hot cross bun in lieu of a cake. I was touched by their warmth, but the exciting presence of the falls had an impact as great as achieving this major goal.

Victoria Falls roared like constant thunder—the natives have a word for it that means "smoke that thunders"—as an awesome volume of water dropped 283 feet along a mile-long narrow gorge, hidden behind a boiling cloud of mist. One crusty old American was heard to say, "Compared to Victoria Falls, Niagara is mere perspiration."

The power of the falls was overwhelming when I walked along the edge of the gorge late that night. Under a full moon I was drenched by the spray, thrilled by the whirling mist and the dancing moonbow.

I finally left the show for a few hours of sleep before returning to see the sun rise through the pinwheeling mist.

Later, in the dense rain forest that borders the gorge, I walked beneath a troop of baboons just waking. They reminded me of humans stretching an arm, yawning, rolling over and curling into a comfortable position for a bit more sleep.

Now it was time to face my long delayed worrying about how to leave Rhodesia. My situation was distinctly unpromising. Overland travelers to South Africa were required to hold an air ticket to their home country and post a $300 to $1,000 bond to insure that they do not become a burden on the state. I emptied my money belt, searched through my wallet and all pockets, and counted my souvenir coins. My total worth came to $32.14. I couldn't transfer any of my emergency money because of the sanctions against Rhodesia. My bank letter would be considered suspect since it was more than a year old. I had met young travelers who had been turned back at Biet Bridge and heard of others stranded on the bridge, teetering, unable to get into South Africa, unable to get back into Rhodesia.

Suddenly the thought occurred, why not fly? Air travelers are never as suspect as overlanders, and I could get help more easily from the Johannesburg airport than from Biet Bridge, 300 miles from the nearest embassy. It was a great idea except for one thing: me and my $32.14. But my new camera had only seen six months of wear. I hopped on the bike, rode into town, offered the camera to a photo dealer whose first offer of R$40, or $75 U.S., was 50 percent more than I had paid for it new in Singapore six months before. Now I had money enough for a ticket to Johannesburg with $17 left over.

The allowable baggage on this economy flight was fifteen kilograms, and the bike and saddlebags weighed thirty-two kilograms. For the first time on my whole world trip, the girl at the desk weighed everything. Then she smiled, wished me well and waved me through. Ready or not, South Africa, here I come.

Chapter 15

Africa South

At the immigration barrier in South Africa it looked touch and go there for a few fluttery minutes. I tried to affect the bloated air of a traveling business mogul, which is hardly my natural style, moving with a brisk confidence as I approached a potty, aging, red-faced immigration official who asked to see my visa and bank letter.

He flipped through the documents with a weary despair. "This letter is out of date," he said. "Let me see your pocket money."

It was plainly time to toss some balls in the air. "Well, I don't have much, not with me, I mean, but more is to be sent along to me here in Johannesburg. Besides, of course, I will be staying with friends until it arrives."

The immigration man was a professional. He cut right through these verbal arabesques, got right down to the bone.

"But where do you work?" he asked, his voice flat and officious.

"Oh, I happen to have my own business back home. I lecture at various universities, I write and I travel extensively."

His face blank, he broke his pencil lead twice pounding it onto the desk in frustration. But then the bicycle arrived, and his face creased in a wide encouraging smile. "Is this your bicycle? And you've been to all those countries? And you didn't get killed in Tanzania? Then you'll be perfectly all right in South Africa."

He stamped the visa, softly shoved the visa and bank letter across the desk and cheerfully wished me luck. It was fortunate I was riding something more than my thumb.

I slept in the airport lounge, and next morning I cycled the express-way into Johannesburg. I had to earn money for the first time in nearly a year and earn it fast. My emergency funds at home still had to be a last resort.

The University of Witwatersrand agreed to a lecture which provided some spending money. The University of Pretoria agreed to a lecture, which bought a new camera. But the Computer Society, my very best hope, was afraid to do anything with art. I wrote three articles, one on my bicycle trip, one on computer art, and one on the Mount McKinley climb, and took them to *Personality*, a general interest magazine, hoping they might buy one of them. To my delight they bought all three, giving me more than enough money to cycle 1,000 miles on to Capetown.

Johannesburg was surprisingly clean and quiet, for so large a city. Cycling through its streets was easy, and people were usually friendly and courteous. Only the strict racial separation policies made it un-pleasant, vulgar, bad. Once I accidentally got on a "non-whites only" bus. The driver refused to go. Every face was frowning. I didn't realize what I had done wrong until a lady informed me that this bus was not for whites. I said that I didn't mind. "But we do," shouted several people at once.

I cycled forty miles north to Pretoria to give my lecture. When I first called the University one of the professors invited me to dinner at his house before he even knew why I was calling. He arranged com-puter time to create some new drawings, talked long into the night about politics in South Africa. Personally, he was against the apartheid policies but admitted, in the interest of self-preservation, there was little else the greatly outnumbered whites could do. "Some people say that our early settlers made a mistake by educating and Christianizing the natives instead of mass killing them as the settlers in America did the Indians and the settlers in Australia did the aborigines." I'd never thought of it quite that way.

After my lecture a friend suggested that instead of fighting South Africa's winter, I should be enjoying Europe's spring. Sure, why not? I could now afford the $500, ninety-day round-trip ticket. I would fly to Europe, cycle around it in its pretty, pretourist season, climb Mont Blanc, fly back to Johannesburg for South Africa's spring, cycle to Capetown in time to crew on the Cape-to-Rio yacht race, cycle across South America and climb Aconcagua. It was a brilliant plan.

I definitely decided to do it, but as I walked to buy the ticket, I nearly collapsed with excruciating internal pains. Within half an hour I had all the same symptoms as had attacked me in Java: headache, diarrhea, fever, porcupine in my torso. I hobbled on to a hospital. A woman doctor there examined me for four hours, tested me for possible diseases, without finding the cause of the trouble. She wasn't amused when I told her how Mbok Nah had healed me of a similar illness in five minutes: "Well, go on out here to Soweto and find yourself a witch doctor if you want to." The examination charge of three rands, or $4.50 U.S., was my only medical bill during the entire four-year trip.

When I showed no sign of recovery after five days' illness, I admitted my excursion to Europe was off. Reverting to my plan of cycling directly to Capetown, I recovered completely.

I planned to leave next morning, but all night I was haunted by a name in my address book. It belonged to Colin Ellison, who had ordered ten dollars' worth of my prints five years before. It seemed silly to contact him since I had nothing to sell or promote or to offer him. Why waste a day of cycling just to make a social call? But nothing would quiet that gnawing feeling except a visit to Colin Ellison.

A pleasant, energetic, balding man, Ellison was glad to see me. He introduced me to his boss, who suggested his company sell my art prints throughout the country. Colin then took me to *Systems Magazine*, where the editor bought a design for use on their cover. Colin climaxed his string of impromptu introductions by presenting me to the chairman of the board; he said the corporation each year commissioned some artist to create several works for their permanent collection. Since one of their subsidiary companies was in the computer business, the chairman's eyes lit up when he heard that I was a computer artist. So did mine when he offered $2,250 for five original drawings of my choosing!

Now I could afford to go all the way home—eventually.

Next morning in the bitter cold air I started cycling straight south toward Lesotho, a small, black-ruled nation surrounded by South Africa. The countryside was flat and heavily farmed, like the prairies of the United States; a strong south wind blasted me right in the face. The traffic was heavy and hostile. To add fuel to a burning depression, my odometer broke, denying me that proof of progress. The only replacement I could buy later measured kilometers instead of miles.

In Lesotho everyone shouted at me. I had to get used to my new name and to the most persistent beggars. The exchanges usually went like this:

"Good morning, baas, how are you?"

"Mean and ornery, how are you?"

"Very well, thank you. Give me money."

"No money."

"Yeah, baas, five cents, please."

In Maseru, the capital city, I wandered about the streets at sunset before stopping at a likely looking flat. Out the door came a big shaggy man with a bushy red beard. "Mister Sumner, I presume," he said. A friend had written Sandy Cairncross two months before that I might be passing through and for him to watch out for me.

Sandy, an Englishman, was working in Lesotho as a water engineer in a program similar to the Peace Corps. I asked how democracy was faring in Lesotho.

"The problem with democracy in most of the new black nations," Sandy said, "is that the power of the presidency is so intoxicating that the ruler will do anything to retain it. Chief Jonathan called an election here a couple years ago to illustrate his strong democratic stand, but when he appeared to be losing during the ballot count, he declared a state of emergency, ruled the election invalid, and is still holding power."

"That's not as bad as Banda in Malawi. He calls his country a great democracy but calls himself the Life President. He even prohibits public discussion of a possible successor for when he dies."

"I think eventually, in twenty to thirty years, a true African system will emerge that is neither democratic nor communist," he said. "Until then, there will be a lot of experimenting and a lot of problems. It's kind of exciting, actually."

Occasionally I asked blacks I met on the road how they felt about life in South Africa, but most just shrugged, afraid to talk or else unaware of any problem. The closest to honest feelings I heard was from one old man who told me, "When white man come, he had the Bibles and we had the land. Now we got the Bibles and he got the land."

Almost predictably, whites were never slow to give an opinion, however fuzzy. "Sure we discriminate," said a jovial, lady storekeeper, "Doesn't everyone? In India they discriminate against the lower castes. Arab and other Moslem countries discriminate against women. Industrial countries discriminate against the poor. Communist countries discriminate against nearly everybody. We discriminate against the blacks. What's the difference?"

At the tourist office in Oudtshorn I met a vivacious widow who loved the area almost as much as she loved helping people. She called a friend and arranged for me to spend the night on his ostrich farm.

At the farm, Ian, a jovial, blond farm worker, showed me around. He said that a 250-pound man could stand on an egg without breaking

The author, always ready to try the unusual, prepares for a ride on the back of an ostrich, Oudtshorn, South Africa.

Arrival at the Atlantic Ocean at Capetown, South Africa. Table Mountain rises above Capetown on a rare smoggy day.

it and that during the incubation period, the male sat on the eggs at night and the female sat by day. I asked about a ride on one of the birds. He was reluctant, which wasn't surprising. After all, he'd fallen off twenty-six of the thirty times he tried himself. Besides, a person can be seriously injured, even killed by the powerful kick of the ostrich, he warned.

Ian placed a cap over the ostrich's head so I could mount. I gripped a wing in each hand, clamped ankles around her thighs, and Ian removed the cap. She bolted straight for the fence, swerved at the last moment and crashed, strong as any fullback, through a group of other birds. The ride was hard and bouncy, and I whopped like a rodeo champion. In the clear my two-legged mount picked up her pace, approaching top speed of forty miles per hour as if my weight were unnoticeable. After the second lap around the field, I jumped off, exuberant that I had survived one more new way of traveling.

A black farm worker who noticed my surprising prowess on the ostrich suggested that I trade him my bike for one of the big birds. I whimsically told him I might consider it if only I knew how to guide an ostrich. "Easy," he said, "just reach up your hand and turn its head what way you like to go." He jumped up onto an ostrich to demonstrate the steering mechanism. But no matter which direction he turned its head, the bird kept pelting straight toward a small lake where it waded in and stood for ten minutes with the helpless passenger kicking and screaming to no avail. Despite the occasional trouble over the long road behind me, my bike looked like first-class transportation.

Four days later I pedaled to the top of Du Toits Kloof Pass and saw Table Mountain of Capetown dominating the southern horizon. From the pass the ride was fast and thrilling, with drops of 2,600 feet around hairpin curves under great vertical cliffs. I rode flat-out through vineyards and heavy freeway traffic to emerge, finally, at Milnerton just in time to see the sun set on the Atlantic Ocean. So I had cycled across my fourth continent, which wasn't bad. Now completion of the whole tour was within reach.

Africa as a whole had been anticlimactic—or else I had become less impressionable, more jaded. Aside from the ostrich ride, South Africa had failed to provide any kicks. Except for the climb of Kilimanjaro, black Africa simply left a big empty void. The culture was not as interesting as that in Asia. Nor did the wildlife excite me like the more elusive animals of Asia and Australia. But maybe it was me. Maybe I had been on the road too long.

Now I looked toward Europe, wondered what I would find. Would it be friendly, civilized or just overdeveloped? Would the many bicycling enthusiasts welcome me? I'd find out for myself soon enough now.

Chapter 16

Europe

English customs was a breeze, no questions, no answers, nothing. I rolled into snarling London traffic, still locked in by the slower beat of Africa. The blare of horns and the screech of brakes jolted my mind into the higher plane of the frenzied Western world, but not before two near-collisions. I wasn't off to an especially good start.

Traffic eased some as I sped away from London. Bicycling became pleasant, very pleasant, in fact, when I traveled on the lovely little country roads. England is one great grid of roads. Big roads carry most of the traffic, medium-size roads carry the rest, leaving the small roads with scarcely any traffic at all. I cycled some of these rarely traveled roads north to Cambridge, stopped to visit a dear friend.

Rachel Britton is on the engineering faculty at Cambridge University. I met her on my first trip to Europe. She visited me once at Ridgeway. Her letters cheered me often throughout my trip. While she is neither a serious climber nor a cyclist, she stays refreshingly in tune with reality by ignoring the vanity that plagues so many other women.

Rachel cooked fabulous meals, took me punting on the Cam, introduced me to her friend Ray Ward, who was eager to climb Mont Blanc. Ray not only agreed to lend me the equipment, but also to join me on the climb. Since his holidays started soon, I decided to cycle through part of the Continent before the climb. Next morning I cycled east to Harwich to catch the ship to Holland.

I joined a stream of other bicycles and mopeds on the cobblestone bikeways toward the interior of Holland. I rode along flower-lined canals, past creaking windmills, through quaint villages on the bone-jarring cobblestoned bikeways. When the lanes ended and I took to highways, I found it strange to ride on the right side again. Except in Portuguese Timor, which hardly counts as there was so little traffic anyway, I had ridden on the left for the last two and a half years, ever since American Samoa.

After a leisurely trip across Holland I entered Belgium, where there were fewer bicycle lanes but actually better riding conditions. I had smoother, wider roads. But when I stopped for food I panicked.

I'd walk into shops very thirsty or hungry and walk out dazed but empty-handed. A small cup of coffee was 50 cents, a Coke was 45 cents, a single scoop of ice cream was 65 cents, a small pastry was 75 cents, an overripe banana was 21 cents. Unable to rationalize paying these inflated prices, I pedaled harder to forget my hunger and rolled into Kortjijk, Belgium, just at dark. A Dutchman in the pub where I stopped to ask directions offered me sandwiches and beer, the bartender said I could camp around back. The 146 miles was my second-longest cycling distance ever.

Early next morning I crossed into France, but instead of the thrill of cycling in still another new country, I was fighting depression, and losing the fight, at that. Perhaps I had pushed too hard. But mostly it was the high prices, the thick traffic, the crowded countryside, the unfriendly people that wore me down. Even on the smallest roads traffic was heavy, resting places scarce and directions hard to follow. Frequently I got lost. Most people peckishly refused to speak English, claiming that, although they knew my language, it was my duty to learn theirs. Even in romantic Paris neither the swinging nightlife nor the bountiful culture excited me. After four years adjusting my eyes and ears to the sights and sounds of nature, I found little uplift in the great museums and orchestras.

I stayed in Paris with Isabelle, the apparition of Mount Bromo, and her sister, mother, aunt and grandmother. Isabelle seemed much younger and less compatible than I had remembered from the smoking edge of the Javanese volcano, but the Vuldy ladies, after giving me a hard time for not knowing French, fed me excellent French cooking, showed me the sights of Paris and took me to their beach cottage at Fort Mahon. Their kindness compensated for the rudeness I had encountered earlier.

A few days later at 2:45 A.M. Ray and two of his students, Alan Penn and Richard Petree, met me in Reims, and drove on through the night toward the French Alps. By midafternoon we arrived in Chamonix, the starting point for the climb of Mont Blanc. When we arrived, I

viewed the five-mph congestion and the double prices on everything
and was glad that I never cycled all the way. I was tired from a sleepless night, but now the mountain rose before me, and my spirits rose
with it.

After camping overnight on a ski run we sorted our gear and started
climbing toward the 15,581-foot summit of Mont Blanc, the highest
mountain in Western Europe. I felt great; I had dreamed of this since
Kilimanjaro. We climbed steadily past gorgeous alpine wild flowers
and panoramic views to 10,000 feet, camped on the snow 100 yards
from the Tête Rousse Hut.

My little one-man tent that had served me so well through the rest
of the world was getting old now. A pack frame supported the rear
and an ice ax shakily held the front. I hoped for a quiet night, hoped
fervently, but threatening clouds put a question mark to my hopes.

The roar of a giant, angry dragon far off in the couloir shook me
awake about midnight. I waited helplessly as the storm whipped
through camp, blowing the tents like sails, rising all the time. It struck
harder, screaming down the glacier, bouncing off the ridge, ripping
the canvas violently, blowing rain now, too. I pulled my sleeping bag
tight, hoped the tent wouldn't blow away. But the pack frame was
dislodged, a corner tie broke, another peg pulled out, the tent collapsed. The rain poured, soaking my sleeping bag, turned to hail,
pounding my head. I re-erected the ice ax but couldn't close the zipper.
Rain drove straight in the door, bringing the tent down again.

"Ray, how're you doing over there?" I yelled.

"Surviving, barely surviving. How about you?"

"I'm getting wet."

"So are we, but spirits are high."

No help there, plainly. Lying in a soaking sleeping bag at freezing
temperatures can turn serious. I laughed, cursed my naivete. Neither
tent nor sleeping bag were adequate for these conditions; I had believed so strongly in my luck and in Loga that I had come to the mountain ill equipped. The deafening roar of the winds squelched any hope
of early relief. The temperature dropped; the rain turned to snow, my
shivering became alarming. I had to move.

I told Ray I was going to the hut, and the three of them cheered me
on with a grossly out-of-tune rendition of "Gory, Gory, What a Hel-
luva Way to Die." Grabbing sleeping bag, ensolite pad and boots, I
squirmed out during a lull, jerked the boots on quickly and forged into
the blizzard, hoping to follow a narrow ridge to some rocks that should
lead to the hut. Four steps away and stifling grayness engulfed me.
I wasn't even sure where the tent was. Instinct led me to the ridge,

sleet and snow stinging my face, and the wind repeatedly blew me down. Once I stepped off the edge into looser snow and was in to my hip. My foot came out but the boot remained. Clinging to the ridge, I probed for the hole again. Toes and fingers went numb.

I paused for a moment, listening to the roar of the wind, and wondered if this would be a good time to panic. No, probably not. I found the boot, put it on, and tied it this time. Which way was I going? The ridge was lost. By turning a careful ear to the wind's blast, I reckoned on a direction, and stumbled on a rock. It led to another and to the steep rock ridge that I believed led to the hut. But sleet covered the rocks. I couldn't hold on. I rolled a few paces down the hill, body exhausted. My mind even began to play games, thirsty on the Nullarbor, baking under the Javan sun, running down a lonely beach, swimming in the pond at Ridgeway. The mist parted to reveal a smooth surface, a building, a rounded rock, something. It was a building, not the hut, but a building all the same. Feeling around, I found a door—locked. I beat, clawed, pulled, lost all feeling in fingers.

Thrusting my freezing wet hands against my naked belly, I slowly felt the tingle return to my fingers. Where to now? The hut had to be nearby. I put my head down and plodded, plodded hard. Another building, another door, which opens. The sleeping bag was no drier of course, but I stayed warm enough to stack up a little sleep.

The storm persisted all next day. We gathered what was left of our equipment, moved into the hut. In late afternoon I tested the storm again for a walk.

By nightfall the storm hit with a renewed velocity. The warden's radio predicted continued bad weather. Ray's barometer read "very stormy." The roar outside the window exposed the staying power of the storm. But Ray woke about 4 A.M., glanced out, and shook me excitedly. "It's perfectly clear outside, no rain, no wind. Let's go for the summit!"

Ray and I took turns leading, climbing the ice- and snow-covered rocks of the Gouter Ridge. Above the Gouter Hut, Mont Blanc looks much like the top of Mount McKinley—great humps of snow, giant seracs, overhanging cornices, scalloped ridges, distant peaks. Somehow I felt at home. The sun was brilliant and the air pleasant.

Alan, out of shape and feeling the altitude badly, stopped at 14,000 feet. Ray, Richard, and I carried on slowly. The last approach up Bosses Ridge was especially beautiful, although narrow, very narrow, only wide enough to walk on single file, and the walls on both sides too steep to stand on, even with crampons.

A summit cloud folded round the top, not threatening, more like a woman's flimsy nightie teasing us with sneak views. Gradually, the ridge began descending. We stopped, the small cloud vanished. We were on top, on the very top. The Matterhorn and other great peaks of the Alps pushed through the rising clouds beyond us. Ray blinked hard. For him Mont Blanc was what Mount McKinley had been to me. As for Richard, he vomited, coughing up all the fatigue and chill. So much for subjective reactions to a mountain.

Having done the one thing I wanted to do on the Continent, I returned with Ray to Cambridge, where I began winding down from

The author climbing toward the summit of Mont Blanc with the Aiguille de Boinnassay ridge in the background

the high of my trip without the hassles of language, expense, and crowding.

But I didn't stay for long. Rachel was leaving for a singing tour of Belgium and Germany, the bike was tilting hard to the west.

With a book of detailed maps I set out to drift around the British Isles. The days were long, the temperature abnormally hot. The English, proud of their sunshine, if only because it was fairly rare, congratulated me on how lucky I was to have such good weather.

The tiny, untraveled roads were often shaded from the sun, which allowed me to cycle through the heat of the day beneath a canopy of foliage. Where there were no trees, tall, thick, interwoven hedgerows blocked the wind and provided shade when I stopped.

England has a great durable look to it. The houses are solid, the gardens neat. Billboards, junk, or tacky buildings don't litter the countryside. It is easy to find a place to camp.

Still, life balances out, even in England. It is not so easy to find a place to answer the call of nature. The hedgerows were impenetrable, solid rock walls were covered with blackberry briars. Once when the situation became rather urgent and the walls remained forbidding, I opted for the side of the road. Why not? I thought. I heard the approach of a car, but not the two small girls on horseback, followed closely by their mothers, who, fortunately, passed quickly.

I cycled on across England and into Wales, where, south of Brecon, I found my favorite cycling conditions. The roads were about five feet wide and billiard-table smooth. There were overlapping trees, cool streams, mountain views, and no traffic. I was often lost, always contented. Further along on another little road I wound peacefully alone for hours through a deep, quiet forest to emerge eventually at a castle.

From Fishguard I sailed to Ireland, where more little roads and more bright sunshine made cycling a daily average of seventy miles and camping every night a great pleasure. Gentle, mellow days melted into memory: the sunrise, waving to farmers on donkey-drawn carts taking milk to market, cycling past fields of haystacks, friendly people, plentiful raspberries and blackberries, sunsets from my solitary camp high on a seacliff.

My route in Ireland took me across the southern end, around the southwest corner, up the west coast to the Cliffs of Moher, northeast toward Larne. Soon after crossing into Northern Ireland a car full of concerned businessmen stopped and asked, "Do you realize where you are?"

"Yes, I believe this is Northern Ireland."

"And you are not afraid?"

"Why should I be?"

"There's trouble, lots of trouble. Two or three people killed every day."

"And how many are not killed each day?"

"What? Oh, about two million, I guess."

"Pretty good odds, wouldn't you say."

The people of the countryside remained friendly, but towns and cities showed grim scars of the war. Houses had been burned, police held machine guns with nervous fingers as they inspected vehicles going into city center.

Nearing Larne, I cycled on a gravel road, the only one I found in the British Isles. Although this road was on my map, it showed no sign

Typical traffic on a typical road that I cycled in Ireland

of other traffic. Only wandering sheep and hopping hares shared my early morning drift across the countryside. After awhile the road ended, snap, just like that. Behind lay at least five miles to a turn-off that could lead only to a heavily traveled expressway.

Certain no one would ever know, I carried the bike over the various obstacles, straining a few muscles on some of the tricky maneuvers. As I began cycling across the sheep pasture, I looked up. Over the horizon came a figure too tall to be a sheep. The farmer was coming straight for me. And what was that long slender thing in his hand?

"Good morning," I said jovially. "Lovely day."

"Good morning," he answered. "Sure need rain, though."

"Say, do you mind if I take your picture?"

He drew himself up, proud and tall, carefully positioning his cane, and called his dog beside him. "Shoot away. That picture will go farther than I ever will." He wished me luck and good health, told me how to find my way out of the field at the other end.

A fast ride down a steep hill brought me to Larne, where I cycled right on board the ship to Stranraer, Scotland.

Camp at Ballantrae, Scotland. This is the one-man, one-pound tent carried all around the world. Maria supports the rear, the flagstaff supports the front, and the spare tire holds out the sides.

Expressing the freedom of the spirit gained from bicycling around the world, the author climbs a sea stack on the Isle of Skye in Scotland to survey the world around him.

The highlands and islands of Scotland are ruggedly beautiful but the roads are crowded, at least in the summer. I cycled up the misty, rocky coast to Ayr, met Rachel for a more extensive tour of Scotland. We climbed in the Cullins of Skye, walked through the mysterious Quirang area, canoed past the sea cliffs of Diabaig, searched for the Loch Ness monster, and tried our hand at fishing.

Rachel is an excellent companion, a strong walker, a gourmet cook, a good conversationalist, easy-going, understanding, emotionally mature. Her kindness put the finishing touches to my winding down process. Except for her deep love for her singing groups and my deep love for adventure, who knows. At least we each gave freely with no enduring expectations.

A few days later Geoffrey Butlin, a friend with a brilliant—and pragmatic—mind, asked, "Just what did you prove by riding a bicycle around the world?"

"I proved a person can accomplish a major goal without outside assistance, can live an exciting, meaningful life without damaging the environment, he can become wealthy by reducing his needs rather than by accumulating money."

"But what did you learn or discover that will help you or the rest of the world? Like Moses you've been to mountain and beyond. Where is the new set of Commandments?"

"Well, I did learn some rules for myself, if not the world. I discovered that the purpose of living is to learn as much as possible through experience. I discovered that there is no such thing as luck, every person gets what he deserves in every situation. I discovered that the human mind is not capable of creative thought; like a computer, it can only feed back results based on what has been fed in. Most importantly, to paraphrase Thoreau, I learned that in wildness is the preservation of the human soul."

"That's pretty heavy stuff. What proof do you have?"

"None, of course." I had no proof that would stand up in court, but I had a strong gut feeling.

I received a shock when I picked up the nonrefundable, specific flight ticket. I was committed to returning to the States. My beautiful trip was slipping away, slipping away.

At Kennedy International Airport in New York, the customs officials were all smiles when they saw my fully loaded bicycle. Their only questions were friendly. How had I enjoyed my trip? No searching, no hassle. They went so far as to volunteer suggestions where I might spend the night, asked if I needed any other help. Maybe the United States was going to be all I hoped.

The Return

I arrived back in the states after spending only $9,915, all of which I had earned along the way. At Kennedy Airport in New York I rolled my round-the-world bicycle through the last maze at Customs, rolled it through the double doors opening into the reception lounge. A cheer rose over a packed crowd, echoed, lingered in space. If it felt like home, well, indeed it was.

I searched the crowd roped off at the end of the passageway for old familiar faces I knew from years ago. In time I saw them too—Mary Machuzak, her long auburn hair cropped close now, smiling from ear to ear, and John Shell, a free spirit I had roved the Virginia hills with, who had waved good-bye the day I left.

Somehow it seemed especially appropriate for these two to be there on my return, offering up a welcome home, playing the old music, once and future friends. Mary, my favorite girl for such a long time, was the only person who might have dissuaded me from embarking on the adventure in the first place. It was awkward picking up the pieces of our lives again in the airport. But she did hint that she might be able to join me on a substantial trip somewhere or other when she completed her master's degree in wildlife management a few months later.

If nearly four years riding the rim of the world had changed me some, the change in John was greater still. We had hiked the hills together, worked a garden, watched the sunrises, swum a pond even when it was so cold we had to crack the ice first. Now he was attending

Bible school in Brooklyn, bound for wherever God might direct him, while he drove a taxi to make ends meet.

"Good old Lloyd." John's face set in that lopsided old grin. "What next?"

"Well, first I have to ride three hundred and fifty miles back to Charlottesville. Then I have to find a place to squirrel away for the winter and write a book. Then—who knows? I might just take off on another trip traveling the world not just by bike but by as many different kinds of transport as I can manage. Want to join up, John?"

"No, but thanks. I'll be too busy doing the Lord's work. You're not tired of all the travel by now?"

"The more I travel, the more I want to travel." I picked my words carefully. "The more I see, the more I realize I haven't seen."

I cycled out of New York into the most magnificent Indian summer I could remember. There was spun gold along the lesser roads I traveled. Since I wanted to enjoy this last leg of the trip as much as any other, I was thankful for the weather. The air crackled, the wind stirred only slightly, the sun lighted the painted land.

On that last leg of the trip the people seemed friendlier, kinder and more understanding, except for one truck driver who intentionally pulled his rig out in front of me and forced me off the road and onto a gravel shoulder. I reacted by abusively shouting at the driver. He snarled back, stopped his truck, came swaggering toward me with his hands balled into fists. The closer he came, the bigger he looked. When it was obvious he was big enough to play professional football, if only he could remember the signals, I hopped on my bike and hastily rode away.

Pumping faster and faster, covering all the distance I possibly could on roadways running clear of major cities, I rode through parts of New Jersey and Pennsylvania, crossed into Maryland, saw the soft curve of Mid-Atlantic America. Before dawn one day I spun into Frederick, Maryland, stiff with history, all red brick and white shutters, so wonderfully picturesque I couldn't help but pause for a long look.

I didn't encounter much traffic on U.S. 340 south except for a police car that bore down on me, lights flashing, siren wailing. Convinced I had done nothing wrong, I pulled over expecting a friendly chat about bicycling, the weather, football. Out of the car came an intimidating-looking policeman, big, wide across the shoulders, his face stern and reproving, already starting to scratch at a ticket form.

"Let's have your driver's license, boy," he said flatly.

"I don't have one, but here is my passport."

Obviously he had never seen a passport before.

"The Secretary of State," he read aloud, "requests all whom it may concern to permit this citizen . . . to pass without delay or hindrance . . . Oh, you a friend of Mister K?"

"Yes, in a manner of speaking," I said.

On hearing that he reduced the ticket to a verbal reprimand, informed me that all controlled access highways, interstate and otherwise, specifically including U.S. three-four-oh, are prohibited to cyclists.

I abandoned the verboten highway for the frontage road at an entrance ramp. Now I was getting so close I could almost smell the sweet Virginia land. The whirling wheels of the bike sang a haunting song: Take me home, country roads.

Halfway across the muddy Potomac I saw the sign. It was blue, showing the red cardinal and white dogwood blossom, the familiar old symbols of Virginia. I rode lightly traveled roads, some of them running along the Shenandoah River, others slanting high in the Blue Ridge Mountains.

At Front Royal, Virginia, I bought a few essentials, climbed into the dusk along the Skyline Drive. The leaves were colorful in the lower area, but a wedge of moon in a sky salted with stars beckoned me higher, higher still, where the leaves thinned out and the air cooled.

A young raccoon skinned up a small tree along a back road. Around a curve a herd of deer stood etched in the twilight. I was home now, home among friends, home to the sights and sounds I hadn't forgotten.

I was tired now, so tired I could hardly spin the wheels, and yet I had to ride the moonlight more. Even after eighty miles of riding the slants of the hills I couldn't fall asleep right away in a makeshift camp in a stand of oak and hickory. There was too much to brood on, too much to treasure. Next day I cycled the Shenandoah National Park, bigger than I remembered, an impressive area. I saw squirrel and deer, ground hog and wild turkey. Most of all I saw me, I suppose, as a boy moving through the Virginia countryside, years and years before.

During a long twelve-hour night there in the park I lay awake as much as I slept. It would be finished in another day, no more, the trip rusting into memory, although that would be more than enough to feed on. The memories were woven of jungle mountains in Sumatra, the Nullarbor Plain in Australia, active volcanoes, sailing stormy seas in the dark of the night, seeing the Royal Bengal tiger close up, rafting the Colorado, watching the sun rise on the rim of Kilimanjaro and other experiences, footprints of an eclectic, speckled world. I had no regrets, no regrets at all.

The author's arrival at Ridgeway, completing a two-wheel trip around the world, November 7, 1975

I slept with my face to the east so the first hint of paling would waken me. I forgot about breakfast, forgot about everything except what lay ahead. I soaked in as much as I could on the final eight miles of Skyline Drive.

Soon the tumble of hills melted away. Traffic may have been thick or thin, either one; I wasn't even aware of it as the miles ran down. I turned south onto Seminole Trail, stopped for the sort of downhome breakfast—hotcakes and grits—I used to savor in my mind half a world away.

I spun the bike onto a small country road, drifting, drifting, over the hills, across the creek, around the bends I remembered again, until I saw a small elliptical sign I had pictured too many times in too many far-off places. "Ridgeway," the lettering read.

The bike rolled down the start of the long drive, across a new bridge that hadn't been there in the autumn of 1971. Hello, trees, here I am. Fence, you tattered old fence, you need mending still. My throat constricted some, my vision temporarily wasn't what it ought to have been.

Moments later, Colonel Blue, looking no older than when I left, came pushing out of the big house to make me welcome. He and Marion, lively and talkative as ever, proudly showed off the changes, the additions, the renovations at Ridgeway.

I strolled the hills I loved, strolled the riverbank. It was pure reflex when I got to the pond. I stripped off my clothes, jumped in for a long swim, climbed out to lean against a tree in the sunshine getting a good grip on my emotions.

As I sat in the warmth of a memorable day I couldn't help but summon up pride for what I had done. But I realized the great blessing of the trip wasn't so much the accomplishment, although that was part of it, or the many wonders I had seen, although they were part of it too. The secret, the secret most people I talk with seem to miss, is the fact that I'd been living every day on an unstructured close-to-nature level.

I have been stretched, in other words, stretched beyond any singing of it. Now I'm as much at home in the Himalayas as in the plains of East Africa, in the sea off Java as in the crowds of urban India. It's a fascinating world spinning out there—and I, for one, don't want to get off. If things work out, I might just see you next time around.

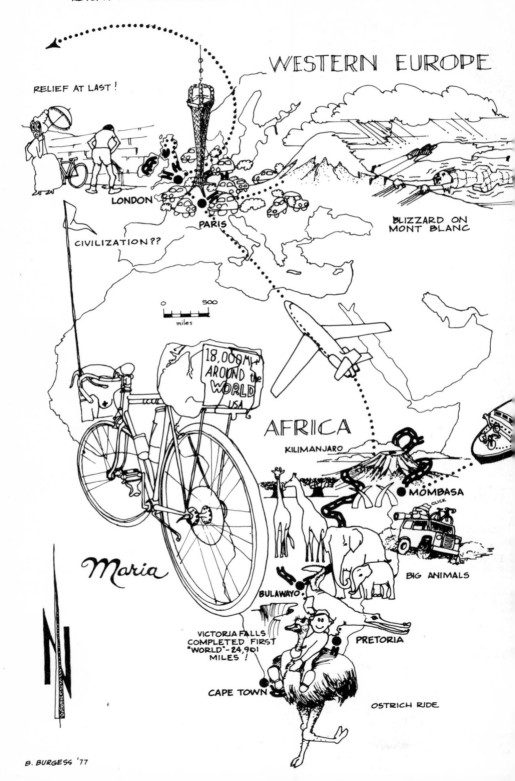